RUMI
BIOGRAPHY AND MESSAGE

RUMI
BIOGRAPHY AND MESSAGE

Cihan Okuyucu

New Jersey

Copyright © 2007 by Tugra Books
Originally published in Turkish as *Mevlana* in 2007
22 21 20 19   2 3 4 5

Published by Tugra Books
335 Clifton Ave
Clifton, NJ, 07011, USA

www.tugrabooks.com

Library of Congress Cataloging-in-Publication Data

Okuyucu, Cihan.
Rumi : biography and message / Cihan Okuyucu.
    p. cm.
Includes bibliographical references and index.
ISBN 978-1-59784-116-0 (pbk.)
1. Jalal al-Din Rumi, Maulana, 1207-1273. I. Title.
PK6482.O42 2007
891'.5511--dc22

                                        2007032760

ISBN: 9781597841160

CONTENTS

INTRODUCTION

B alkh 1207 and Konya 1273... These years mark the beginning and end of the great Sufi Master Jalaladdin Rumi. He was born eight centuries ago, and passed away 734 years ago; but he had discovered the secret of a birth to immortality. In spite of the centuries that passed after his death, this blessed figure is still among us with his never-fading message. Not every mortal is so fortunate to have such a prolific life. Time obliterates many great figures from memories, but the name of Rumi becomes ever brighter as time passes. The halo of love forming around that blessed message continues to grow. The river of love that has incessantly flowed for eight centuries will hopefully find new mouths that will drink from it today and new hearts to revive it; Unesco has declared 2007 to be the Year of Rumi.

What can be the source of the growing interest in Rumi? How has he drawn so much interest? Maybe the answer lies with the following words of A.J. Arberry: "Viewing the vast landscape of Sufi poetry, we see him standing out as a sublime mountain peak; many other poets before and after him are like hills in comparison."

The historian Joseph von Hammer described the *Masnawi* as the pocket book for all Sufis, from the banks of the river Ganges to the shores of the Bosphorus. Though not mistaken, this definition needs to be broader, now that the message of Rumi has reached overseas. In his *Masnawi*, Rumi states that along with physicians who only cure physical diseases, there are doctors who cure spiritual diseases. According to Arberry, this spiritual doctor is Jalaladdin Rumi. He sees Rumi's works as the potential cure for Europeans. Likewise, Irene Melikoff suggested that if the nations of the world were to translate Rumi's works into their languages and read them, there would be no evil or war, no grudges or hatred in the world. Though Rumi was born in Balkh and buried in Konya, the map of his heart covered a much larger area. He transcended time and place to embrace everyone with a welcoming heart. After all, how many people are there in world history have been able to take the sky as their roof and the entire humanity as their family!

Rumi, a true inheritor of the Messenger who was sent to all humanity, spoke a transcendent language. Like a pair of compasses, he had one foot fixed on his own values, and then he embraced all nations, which he took as the manifestation of the Light of God. Muslims saw the teachings of the Prophet Muhammad embodied in him; at the same time he represented the teachings of Jesus for Christians, and those of Moses for Jews. A mature mind and an enthusiastic heart were united in him. This is why he has satisfied both hearts and minds up to the present. As a call to goodness, the echo of his voice is still heard. We can say what he said about Shams for Rumi himself:

Spill water on the roads,
Give glad tidings to the gardens
The smell of spring is coming,
He is coming—it is "he!"
Our bright moon, the dear one is coming.
Let him pass, make way, disperse!
Stand aside all of you!
His face is radiant, so pure,
Illuminating everywhere he walks,
He is coming—it is "he!"

This book has been prepared to commemorate the "Year of Rumi." The first two chapters are about the life and works of Rumi. Although some main sources have been referred to, the book is intended to be an informative study rather than an academic one. The parables in the final chapter are taken essentially from the *Masnawi* and *Fihi Mafih*; they can be considered as guidelines that reflect Rumi's philosophy.

Cihan Okuyucu
Fatih University, April 2007

CHAPTER 1

A LIFE OF LOVE AND WISDOM

THE MAIN SOURCES ABOUT RUMI

There are many figures in the history of Islam about whom we know very little. In this respect, Jalaladdin Rumi is exceptional, since we have a rich body of literature about his life. His life and thoughts have been the subject of many works, owing both to the significance of the family he belonged to and the great influence he had. We would like to briefly introduce the sources that will be used before telling his life story. Definitely the best sources for all outstanding figures are their own works. Unfortunately, Rumi hardly ever talks about himself in his works. If we put aside the secondary sources, there are three main sources about Rumi which are available to contemporary researchers. Here are the names of these authors and their works:

I) Sultan Walad: Waladnama, or Ibtidanama.

Sultan Walad, who was Rumi's son and his successor, gives limited information about his father in some of his writings. *Ibtidanama*, which he wrote in 1291, and which imitated his father's style, has special significance. It consists of ten thousand couplets. Although the objective was to tell about Rumi and those around him, the author preferred to focus on didactic themes, thus making biographical information secondary. The information given is reliable, but the fact that it is brief and scattered throughout the work makes it difficult for the researcher.

II) Faridun b. Ahmad Sipahsalar: Risala of Sipahsalar

Beginning in his childhood, the author served Rumi for 40 years. He started writing the story of Rumi and the people around him, but after his death in 1312, his son completed the last part of the text. The book recounts Rumi's life, beginning with Rumi's father, Bahauddin Walad, and includes prominent figures such as Ulu Arif Chelebi and Abid Chelebi. In comparison to the plain narrative of Sultan Walad, Sipahsalar adopted the style of Farideddin Attar's *Tazkiratul Awliya* and wrote his work in parables. In this respect, the information he gives needs to be approached carefully.

III) Aflaki: Manaqibul Arifin ("The Parables of the Sages")

This is the most extensive and well-known source about Rumi. It is narrated that Aflaki, who came to Konya in 1291—quite a long time after the other authors—met Sultan Walad. After that, Aflaki became a disciple of Sultan Walad's son, Ulu Arif Chelebi (d. 1360). At the request of his sheikh, Aflaki started to write his work in 1318, and after more than thirty years, he finally finished it in 1353. Aflaki benefited from Sultan Walad's *Ibtidanama* and other works, as well as making use of the *Risala* of Sipahsalar. He added the narrations of Rumi's surviving friends to what he gathered from these works, and then wrote his voluminous work. Tahsin Yazici finds it more successful in comparison to the other two works with respect to the mastery of the language and the richness of the information presented. However, Yazici also criticizes *Manaqibul Arifin* for the abundance of mistakes and exaggerations. Therefore, a significant part of Yazici's study has been devoted to showing these errors. Actually, there are several facts in these three works that conflict with one another, making research more difficult. In addition to these three main documents other modern research has been used. In particular, *The Encyclopedia of Islam*, by DVIA (Turkish Ministry of Religious Affairs) and Furuzanfar's valuable work, *Mawlana Jalaladdin*, can be mentioned among these. In spite of making extensive use of sources, the aim of this book is not to be a purely academic study; as much as possible we have tried to avoid disputed matters and present facts that are generally accepted.

HIS EARLY LIFE

Balkh

Sanctify Balkh, O you passers by
It is the city where the best of cups was filled one day.

Today, a traveler who is able to go to Northern Afghanistan with the intention of seeing Rumi's hometown will probably experience great disappointment when they see the narrow and gloomy streets formed by the adobe houses of Balkh, which now rather resembles a large town. They will probably have difficulty in believing that this desolate city, where one can find no more than a few traces, here and there, of ancient *madrasa*s (Islamic schools) and tombs, once used to be one of the most luminous cities of Khorasan. This same visitor is sure to ask, then, whether this place really used to be the intellectual and religious center that cherished great figures like Sultan Walad and Jalaladdin Rumi. Certainly, what most strikes the traveler is the dramatic difference between the contemporary state of the city and its glorious past. Indeed, after being conquered in 663 CE during the reign of the Caliph Muawiya, control of the city shifted between different dynasties and it constantly developed. When Rumi was born, the city was in its heyday and merited the title, "the Dome of Islam," with its lively trade, splendid *madrasa*s, and numerous scholars and spiritual figures. Along with the vibrant academic life, there was a strong Sufi atmosphere prevalent in the city. This was the place where the great Sufi masters Ibrahim Adham and Shaqiq al-Balkhi had lived in the past. Najmeddin Kubra (1145-1221 CE), the sheikh of the Kubrawi order, was still alive when Rumi was a child. However, a disaster awaited the city. After Baha Walad, Rumi's father, and his family left the city, the Mongolian invasion reached the city and all the inhabitants were put to the sword. The destruction was so great that when the famous traveler Ibn Battuta came to the city nearly a century later, he found that it was still in ruins. Later on there were attempts to revive the city by the Chagatay, Uzbek, Persian, and Afghan rulers—yet it never returned to its glorious past.

Baha Walad

Rumi's father Baha Walad belonged to a family which had raised scholars for many generations. His father, Bahaeddin Walad, was a respected scholar and a Sufi figure known as the "sultan of scholars." According to Sipahsalar, who later related the story of this family, Bahaeddin Walad was a disciple of Najmeddin Kubra who refused to flee the city during the Mongol raids and heroically fought until his last breath with his loyal disciples. Najmeddin Kubra was the great sheikh of the Kubrawi Sufi order, which can be traced back to Ahmad al-Ghazzali. The Kubrawi order, a branch of the Shuttar order, provided a way that aimed at spiritual progress and being drawn to God through an ecstatic love of Him. This Kubrawist concept found a place in Rumi's thought, and maintained its influence on him.

It is worth noting that the information given by Aflaki about Rumi's family is usually exaggerated. He asserts that Bahaeddin Walad was the grandson of the Khwarazmian sultan, Alaeddin Muhammad, from his mother's side. However, this is not mentioned in any other source, and this compels us to regard it as fiction rather than fact. Baha Walad married Mumina Hatun, the daughter of the ruler of Balkh, Rukneddin. Their first son was Alaeddin Muhammad, and the second son was Muhammad Jalaladdin—or, as we know him today, Jalaladdin Rumi. In some places, Rumi is also called *Mawlana*, a title meaning "our master."

Although he spent most of his life in Anatolia, Rumi did not forget his hometown. In his texts he often refers to himself as being from Khorasan, which also includes Balkh, and he declares his love for the people of Khorasan. However it should be noted that Rumi does not refer to his own lineage in his works. Sipahsalar and Aflaki also point out that his father, Bahaeddin Walad, was a descendant of the first caliph, Abu Bakr.

The Time and Place of Rumi's Birth

The common belief is that Rumi was born on September 30th, 1207. However, an expression which Rumi himself used in his *Fihi Mafih* makes this doubtful. Rumi gives an account of the siege of Samarkand by the Khwarazmians, and he narrates how a young girl he knew prayed: "O God, do not leave me to the hands of the cruel enemy." Taking this as a starting point, Will Durrant calculates his year of birth as being 1201, and Maurice Barres as 1203. On the other hand, Golpinarli takes one of his poems in *Divani Kabir* as his basis, where Rumi asserts that when he met Shams of Tabriz (1244) he was 62; therefore he must have been born in 1184. However, this assertion is not accepted as reliable by researchers like Helmut Ritter. Although tentatively, the year 1207 is accepted as his year of birth; thus 2007 has been declared to be the 800-year anniversary of Rumi's birth by UNESCO.

The Migration

Rumi was raised in an environment filled with noble and educated people. As he grew up, he was instructed by his father, Baha Walad and his more mature disciples. In accordance with the tradition of the time, two of his father's disciples were responsible for Rumi's education. One of them, Sharafeddin Lala of Samarkand, would later become his father-in-law. The other was his first master after his father's death, Sayyid Burhaneddin. The reports of his childhood years, in the earliest sources, consist only of parables. For instance, Aflaki narrates that even in his childhood years Rumi was in contact with spiritual beings, that he ascended to the heavens together with Sayyid Burhaneddin, etc.

In the happy childhood days of Rumi, his father's relationship with the Khwarazmian sultan and his close environment grew tense. The reason for this was a rivalry between two schools: the Sufi school lead by Baha Walad, and the school of philosophy lead by the great scholar, Fakhreddin Razi. At the beginning, Sultan Alaeddin was inclined toward the Sufi school, but later on he favored Razi. Majdeddin of Baghdad was among the prominent Sufis and he was the chief opponent of Razi. The fact that the sultan had Majdeddin thrown into the Amu Darya River gives the modern observer an idea of just how strong the controversy actually was. In Baha Walad's later compilation of counsels, entitled *Maarif*, and also in the works by Rumi himself, we often come across criticism of philosophers, and particularly of Razi. Under these circumstances, Baha Walad decided to emigrate west with his family, which is commonly accepted as having taken place in 1212—or, according to another view, in 1221. One naturally wonders about the reason for this decision. Aflaki ascribes it to the tension mentioned above, and asserts that the sultan banished Baha Walad from the country because he criticized Razi and the sultan for following Razi. Even though Sipahsalar claims that it was Razi who provoked the sultan against Walad, this is evidently mistaken; Razi was already dead at least three years before this emigration. During their emigration, the age of Rumi again appears as a problem. Aflaki takes the year 1212 and asserts that he was five or six. On the other hand, Sultan Walad's account asserts that Rumi was fourteen at the time. Again, Sultan Walad does not talk about the above-mentioned tension and just explains that his grandfather's emigration was precipitated by his being offended by the people of Balkh, and by a spiritual sign he received urging him to go to the Hejaz. Nicholson and Ritter are of the opinion that the family left Balkh in order to flee the Mongolians. Indeed, historical accounts show that in those days wealthy families emigrated from Balkh toward the west, to lands they thought to be more secure—so much so that even the rents in Baghdad increased excessively due to overcrowding.

On the Way

As we have mentioned already, Sultan Walad, Faridun Sipahsalar, and Aflaki give contradictory data about the emigration from Balkh and the trip to the Hejaz. Therefore, instead of elaborating on the dates, we will just inform the reader about the itinerary followed. Baha Walad, who traveled with his family and disciples, was welcomed with great interest at every city he stopped in. In Nishabur, which was the first stop after Balkh, they were met by Farideddin Attar (d. 1221 CE), one of the famous Sufi figures of the time. Like Baha Walad, Attar was a Kubrawi who had been taught by Najmeddin Kubra, and he thus had a special interest in Walad. However, after they met, Attar's interest turned to the son rather than the father. The old sheikh sensed the potential of the young Rumi and gave him his work entitled *Asrarnama* ("The Book of Mysteries"). This encounter had a lasting effect on the young Rumi. In his famous *Masnawi* he took some of his stories, such as the merchant and the parrot, from Attar's work. In conformance with Sultan Walad's account, we can infer that Rumi was probably fourteen, as it makes more sense for Attar to present his work to a young man than to a child who was probably not capable of reading such a work. The second important stopover of the caravan was in Baghdad, the center of the caliphate. The arrival of this foreign group drew much attention. What raised even more interest was the answer Baha Walad gave to those who asked where they were coming from and where they were heading: "We come from God, and to Him again we return." These words went round the city, and they reached the famous Sufi, Shahabeddin Suhrawardi, who recognized the person who said these. He said, "no one but Baha Walad could have uttered these words." Then Suhrawardi set forth, ran to meet Baha Walad, and kissed his knees. The people of the caravan were looking forward to completing the pilgrimage, and they only stayed for three days. Before they left the city, travelers from Khorasan brought bad news: the Mongols had invaded Balkh.

It is known that the cities of Khorasan were invaded by the Mongols in 1220-21, and thus we can confirm the time when the caravan was in Baghdad. The accounts given about their return are contradictory again, but their point of agreement is that the first stopover on their return from the Hejaz was in Damascus. It can be understood that Baha Walad did not waste much time in Damascus. He moved on to Erzincan—which was ruled by the Mengucek sultan, Fakhreddin Bahramshah—via Malatya and Sivas, according to Aflaki. After staying there for a while, Baha Walad proceeded to Malatya, and then to Larende (Karaman). Amir Musa, the Seljuk Governor of Karaman, welcomed him with due respect and had a *madrasa* built for his famous guest—who only would stay at *madrasa*s along the way. Their stay in Larende, which was rather long in comparison to their other stops—seven years according to Aflaki—had an important place in Rumi's life. In 1225, he married his teacher's daughter, Gawhar Hatun. In the same year, the family suffered two losses. Rumi's mother, Mumina Hatun and his brother, Muhammad Alaeddin, passed away, one after the other. Then, two happy events came afterwards: one year after the marriage, their first son, Mehmed Bahaeddin, who would later be known as Sultan Walad, was born; the next year, their second son, Alaeddin Mehmed, followed. Rumi's marriage with Gawhar Hatun lasted for years; after her death, he married in Konya for a second time. He had two more children from his second wife, who was named "Karra" or "Kira." One of them was Muzaffareddin Amir Alim Chelebi, and the other was his only daughter, Malika Hatun. Tahsin Yazici believes that his second wife was Greek. Also, Rumi had a stepson, his second wife's son, called Shamseddin Yahya, who died at a young age.

Now let us return to the time spent in Larende. While there, Baha Walad's reputation kept spreading; in fact, it reached as far as the Seljuk capital. The state was in last stages of its brilliance before the Mongol invasion, and Alaeddin Kaykubat had sat on the Seljuk throne in Konya since 1219. The sultan kept expanding the boundaries of the state, and he took precautions against the approaching danger, the Mongolian invasion. Along with the merits of his leadership, the sultan was fond of the arts and he cared deeply for scholars. Thus, his courteous behavior attracted many scholars and sheikhs to Konya. According to Aflaki, Alaeddin Kaykubat protested at Amir Musa keeping such a great figure in Larende, and invited Baha Walad to Konya. The author has an exaggerated narration of how the sultan met Baha Walad and received him. He even claims that the sultan was ready to abandon his throne to Baha Walad, but Sultan Walad himself does not narrate anything of the sort about his grandfather's arrival.

Baha Walad spent the last two years of his life in Konya, preaching and counseling. He conquered the hearts of the sultan and the people with his lessons in the *madrasa* and his sermons in the mosque. One of his followers, Amir Badreddin Gawhartash, built a *madrasa* for his sheikh and his family.

When the old sheikh died at the age of 85 in 1231, he left behind two significant contributions. One of them was his book, *Maarif*, a compilation of his talks and sermons; the other was his son Rumi. Later on, the book became quite popular among Sufis as it presents the mastery of Baha Walad in both the inward and outward disciplines. The oft-mentioned ideas about Fakhreddin Razi and the Khwarazmian sultan indicate that most of the talks were given prior to Baha Walad's emigration from Balkh. *Maarif*, described by Furuzanfar as an elegant and unique work of prose on the truths of Sufism, was for years one of Rumi's favorites. The similar styles of *Maarif* and the *Masnawi*, and their shared parables—for instance, the parable of the slave named Sungur, and his master going to pray—reveal how Rumi was influenced by his father. Undoubtedly, however, the greatest treasure that Baha Walad left behind was his son; in fact, one could say that it was thanks to Rumi that his father's name is known today.

When his father passed away—according to Aflaki—Rumi was twenty-four years old. We can roughly divide the rest of Rumi's life into two periods: that before Shams and that after Shams. These two periods can also be named as the period of reason and the period of love. Undoubtedly, Rumi's inner quests continued throughout all of the periods of his life. Nevertheless, from 1231 until

1244, when he met Shams of Tabriz, Rumi was regarded principally as a scholar, an ascetic who was striving to embrace the truth. His first master on this path would be Sayyid Burhaneddin Muhaqqiq al-Tirmidhi, one of his father's disciples who had earlier tutored him in Balkh. Actually, Burhaneddin came to Konya to see his sheikh, Baha Walad. On learning of the sheikh's death, Burhaneddin decided to stay in Konya as the spiritual guide of the son. His aim was to help Rumi become a perfected man in terms of the inner and outer disciplines, like his late father. Their relationship lasted for nine years, although they were not together throughout this period. After one year, Burhaneddin sent Rumi to Aleppo and Damascus to attain deeper spirituality. During this journey, which is estimated to have taken place in 1233, Burhaneddin accompanied Rumi from Konya to Kayseri, where he stayed instead of returning. In Aleppo, Rumi took lessons at the *madrasa* of Hallawiya from Kamaleddin Ibn al-Adim, who was also the governor of the city. We are not certain on how long Rumi stayed in Aleppo. His second stopover on the path of learning was Damascus. The city, which was among the most significant cultural centers of the time, certainly bears great relevance in terms of Rumi's progress. During his four years in Damascus, Rumi completed his education in all the major subjects of the day, such as Arab literature, knowledge of the lexicon, Islamic jurisprudence, Qur'anic commentary, and the traditions of the Prophet. At the same time, he had the opportunity to meet the great Sufi masters like Muhyiddin ibn al-Arabi, Saadeddin Hammuya, Uthman al-Rumi, Awhaduddin Kirmani, and Sadreddin Konevi—who were all in Damascus at the time.

When Rumi returned to Kayseri, he had mastered the studies he needed. There was only one thing left to do: retreat for ascetic practice. His master subjected Rumi to three consecutive 40-day periods of ascetic retreat. He went through these periods eating and sleeping very little. In the end, Rumi returned to the outer world purified and with a heart awakened to divine secrets. The master was pleased with the outcome: "Come on!" he said. "Walk forth and bring a fresh spirit to the people. Let them attain over-flowing divine mercy, and revive their hearts with love." After that, he accompanied his disciple as far as Konya, but the master himself would not stay there. On asking why the master refused to stay, Rumi received the following answer: "A lion who set off from Tabriz is coming this way. I am just another lion. Two lions do not inhabit the same place. So now I have to go away."

Burhaneddin died in 1241, a short time after returning to Kayseri. His tomb is still the most-visited one in the city today. In 1241 Rumi, now middle-aged, returned to his post in the *madrasa* as a matured teacher. Though he was allowed by Burhaneddin to be a sheikh and serve as a spiritual guide, he still dressed and acted like an academic. The number of his students increased day by day. As M. Bahari Baytur states, he still had divine love in him, but his love was hidden in his piety. In later periods, his piety would hide in his love. This quiet and routine life continued until 1244 , the year when he met Shams of Tabriz. Shams was the wind that would blow the scholar's turban off from Rumi's head, and turn a quiet academic into an enthusiastic lover of God.

AFTER MEETING SHAMS OF TABRIZ

Shams was called "the flying one," as he had been to so many differ-ent lands, spending nearly all of his life traveling. Although he resem-bled a humble dervish, in reality he was a learned man. His work, *Maqalat*, which was compiled from his sermons, gives us an idea of his substantial knowledge of classic Islamic studies, like Qur'anic commentary and the traditions of the Prophet. Even though there are irregularities due to the fact that the work was compiled from notes taken down, Furuzanfar considers it to be among the best works of prose in Persian literature, in terms of language.

Shams had been in the service of Sheikh Abu Bakr al-Salabaf, and he met with many other Sufis, but neither his own sheikh nor others satisfied his thirst for knowledge. He was a man who was afraid of no one but God, who spoke straightforwardly, and who did not easily approve of any person. In short, he was a fervent and ecstatic Sufi. In Damascus, he reproached Awhaduddin Kirmani and he was unconvinced by Ibn al-Arabi. He was already sixty, but still he continued his quest. The reader might ask, "A quest for what?" Well, it seems that Shams was seeking an even greater fire to put out the fire in himself and more immense and salty oceans to satisfy his thirsty soul. With this longing, he supplicated the Almighty and said: "O God! Please show me one of your disguised lovers." He must have received a sign, as in the end he set upon the road to Anatolia with refreshed hope.

Shams experienced desperate thirst in his quest, but the person he sought was also in need of such a seeker. In a way, Rumi describes this in the following couplet:

> The thirsty moans were craving for the sweet drinking-water
> And the water cries: "Where is the thirsty one?"

Another couplet from the *Masnawi* voices the same reality:

> Whoever you see in love is also a loved one at the same time,
> The thirsty seek for water, but the water is also in love with the thirsty ones...

The arrival of Shams in Konya in this mood, according to Aflaki, was on November 29, 1244. There is contradictory data about how Shams and Rumi met for the first time and what they said. I will try to combine what Sipahsalar and other sources relate about their first meeting.

Rumi had left the *madrasa* and he was proceeding on his mule, conversing with his students, who surrounded him. He suddenly came across Shams on the street. Shams made him stop with a shattering question: "Tell me, who is greater, the Prophet Muhammad or Bayezid al-Bistami?" Rumi reacted, "How can you ask such a thing? Can Bayezid be compared to God's Messenger, Muhammad, peace and blessings be upon him?" Shams insisted, "Then explain to me why God's Messenger said, 'O God, we have not been able to recognize You as You deserve to be recognized,' and asked for God's forgiveness seventy times a day. Yet Bayezid said, 'Glory be to me, how exalted I am.' So who is mistaken here?"

Rumi replied "Here is your answer: Bayezid's thirst was little enough to be satisfied with the drop of water he attained. At the first spiritual level he reached, the capacity of his glass was filled up, and he uttered those words in a state of intoxication. However, the Noble Prophet, who kept ascending seventy spiritual levels every day, could see the pettiness of his previous level at each new level he reached, and sought forgiveness for being content with the former amount. This is the reason." On hearing this, Shams let out a cry and fainted. Rumi held his arm and took him to his *madrasa*. Seemingly, this encounter had a great impact on both. Perhaps Rumi was describing this encounter and the meaning of the piercing looks of Shams when he wrote:

> The moon appeared in the sky at dawn,
> He descended from the sky and looked at me.
> Like a falcon hunting its prey,
> He took me up to the sky.

This is how their friendship began. Unlike the traditional sheikh-initiate relationship, Rumi and Shams became spiritual masters to one another. Sultan Walad made a comparison between the friendship of his father with Shams to that of Prophet Moses and Khidr.[1] As Moses sought Khidr, despite being a prophet, Rumi, too, sought Shams, despite being the greatest scholar of his time. It seems that Shams put his new friend to various tests, much as Khidr tried Moses. Shams seemed to be an eccentric dervish trying to transcend the limits, and he was looking for a person of sound understanding to accept him as he was. In reality, he had a firm conviction concerning the essential truths of Islam, as he expressed in *Maqalat*: "I would not exchange even the (apparently) simplest saying of the Prophet in return for the most valuable books, like the *Risalat of Kushayri*."

Legends always tell us to look for treasure under ruins. Likewise, Rumi reached with his keen insight into the soul of Shams and discovered the ore shining under that ruinous appearance. Therefore, he passed with success all the tests to which Shams' friendship put him, and he became his friend—though friendship

with Shams came at a high cost. In order to reach this man, who had
forsaken the world, and to soar through the same skies with him he
had to leave behind everything he possessed—everything he
described as "mine." No one until then had been able to pay this
cost, but Rumi was an exceptional person. Rumi was a unique scholar of his time and he laid before Shams his knowledge, profession,
and fame—in short, everything he had—obtaining Shams in return.
What did this friendship bring Rumi? What good did it do for
Shams? The following sentences of Golpinarli sum the situation
well: "If Shams had not come, Rumi probably would not have
become what he is; he would have remained as an ordinary sheikh,
just a Sufi among countless others. As for Shams, on the other hand,
if he had not met Rumi, his name would never have been heard.
Rumi had already reached the level at which he could experience such
enthusiasm. He was like an oil-lamp prepared to be lit. All he needed was a spark. This was actually what Shams did. When Rumi started to burn with a dazzling light, Shams became a moth around him,
gave his life, and disappeared into his light."

In consequence, both found what they had been looking for—
like tinder and flint. Rumi spent his time with Shams, continuous-
ly. He neither thought about his lessons at the *madrasa*, nor his students looking for their master. His entire world became Shams,
and Shams alone. At this age and level of perfection, he put aside
everything and knelt before his new master. And the name of this
school was the school of divine love.

Earlier, when Rumi continued to read his father's *Divan*, he
was inspired by Attar's *Masnawi*. Yet, these were the books of others, and the words of others. Shams had seen the potential of the
volcano before him and could not stand seeing Rumi lose time
with the works of others, uttering the words of others. Shams felt
that whatever others had said, Rumi could say more and say it
much better. He only needed to turn to his own heart and listen to
the divine voice of wisdom inspired in his soul. So this is what
Shams helped him to do:

> *You should rely on the bright light in the heart,*
> *Empty tales cannot solve this mystery, knotted tight.*
> *Of little use to you are the rivers in the mountain,*
> *While, at home you have a flowing fountain.*

The two friends remained frozen in time with the ecstasy of gazing at each other's inner paradise, but in the outer world time was flowing for others. Rumi's old friends and his students, who had surrounded him like a halo of love, saw how bad the situation had become, and they became opposed to Shams. This uninvited guest had suddenly come between them and their master, like an arrow falling from the sky. Though "*shams*" means "sun," they saw him as a cloud throwing a shadow on their sun. And Rumi seldom came out; he saw no one but Shams and was loyal to his new friend, even at the risk of going against the rules of society, as the following example demonstrates.

Jalaladdin Karatay, an admirer of Rumi, had a *madrasa* built and brought together there all the great scholars. Shams, who was not a scholar, was given a seat with those of the lowest level among the commoners. They then asked Rumi about which was the best seat. He replied "It depends. For scholars, it is in the middle, for the wise, it is in corner of the home, and for lovers, it is right next to the beloved." After saying that, he sprang to his feet and took a seat near Shams. This was not the only act that caused his friends to feel envy and sorrow. Rumi performed unusual acts which they were not used to seeing. The dignified scholar had before eaten only once every three days and had prayed until morning was past—now there was this enthusiastic dervish. Earlier, Rumi had had no knowledge of the "*sama*"[2] or of music; but now, he would become enraptured and start to clap his hands, whirling along with the touching moaning of the reed flute—the *ney*, and taking flight with the sound of the Sufi violin—the *rabab*. As Shams stayed in Konya even longer, the resentment of the people grew; soon it built up to an intolerable point. In addition, some words of Shams were misunderstood, for they required a certain spiritual level and sound discernment. They just added fire to the flames. Undoubtedly, Rumi was aware of this. One

day, when Rumi was walking with his students, they saw a dog
gnawing a bone and suckling her puppies. He stopped abruptly and
spoke: "Do you know; this picture summarizes the situation we are
in. If those puppies try to eat the bone themselves, they will perish.
The mother eats it, turns it into milk, and feeds her young. It is
impossible for you to swallow the bone-like words of Shams. I do it
for you, and feed you afterwards. So then, you don't need to listen
to him, but listen to me."

On the other hand, Rumi's students were trying the patience
of Shams, who was putting up with all of their harassment for
the sake of Rumi. Finally, Shams, "the flying one," disappeared
all of a sudden, sixteen months after coming. Those who were
happy with his departure soon understood their mistake. The
separation fanned the fire of Shams in Rumi, and matters
became even worse. He was heart-broken and bitter toward
those who had caused their separation, and he withdrew from
people. When he learned that Shams was in Damascus, he sent
four consecutive letters full of emotion, begging Shams to come
back to Konya:

"O the light of our hearts! O the wish of our wishes! O the
one we entrusted our lives to! Please don't prolong this separation!
Please come!" In the end, the pleading had its effect, and Shams
started his journey back to Konya, together with Sultan Walad,
who had come to take him back. Rumi must have uttered the following lines while Shams was still on his way to Konya:

> *Spill water on the roads,*
> *Give glad tidings to the gardens*
> *The smell of spring is coming,*
> *He is coming—it's "he!"*
> *Our bright moon, the dear one is coming.*
> *Let him pass, make way, disperse!*
> *Stand aside all of you!*
> *His face is radiant, so pure,*
> *Illuminating everywhere he walks,*
> *He is coming—it's "he!"*

On the other hand, during this journey, which lasted a month, a strong friendship developed between Shams and Sultan Walad. Shams loved this respectful youth, who took the reins of his horse and traveled on foot, and he revealed his spiritual secrets to him. The first absence of Shams lasted nearly 15 months. The lines below express the joy of Rumi on being reunited with him:

> *He has come, O friends!*
> *My moon, my sun has come!*
> *The silver man, the golden skin!*
> *My eye, my ear, my soul has come!*
> *I am intoxicated,*
> *I feel dizzy today.*
> *The swaying willow has come!*

In order to forgive his students for what they had done, Rumi required them to be forgiven by Shams first. The guilty ones were forgiven and the faded face of Rumi smiled again; everything seemed fine. However, such an appearance was misleading. Rumi's unusual behavior was on the rise again. Not only his behavior, but his clothes changed. He left his scholarly robe and turban, and he wore a woolen cap and a simple *hirqa* (dervish cloak) instead. Shams kept inciting him to the *sama*. The people of Konya were more or less familiar with the *sama,* which had been a point of discussion between Sufis, including Imam Ghazzali. However, they still could not easily accept seeing the greatest scholar in their city whirl along with the music of the *ney* and the *rabab*. However, the *sama* had a different meaning for Rumi. The *ney*, in particular, virtually whispered into his ear the secrets of *Qalu Bala*—man's profession of God's Lordship:

> *Telling the hidden secrets of the world,*
> *The whining ney, the ney!*

Rumi was making up for the time he had lost. In the *madrasa* he conversed with Shams, and for six months he almost forgot the world. Only Sultan Walad and Salahaddin Zarqubi were able to go near them. And if we believe Aflaki's narration, supernatural events happened. One day, when Rumi's wife, Kira Hatun, looked inside, she was puzzled to see six Indian men appear from nowhere near

Rumi and Shams. Later on, Rumi presented his wife with a bunch of flowers brought by those men, and told her not to tell anyone about it. In a couplet, Rumi expresses how he was alienated from everybody else when he was with Shams:

> *I have taken you as my own soul,*
> *I have turned my back to all the people around me for your sake.*

In his *Maqalat,* on the other hand, Shams expressed the meaning of Rumi for him:

> *"I am the demanded one,*
> *But Rumi has become the demand of the demanded one."*

The two souls were burning together with the love of God. In the meantime, Shams married Rumi's step-daughter, Kimya Hatun. It happened at the request of Rumi, probably with the aim of ensuring that Shams would stay in Konya.

However, the enmity against Shams became incited once again due to this long absence of Rumi and the premature death of Kimya Hatun. Some narratives include Rumi's younger son, Alaeddin Chelebi, among these enemies. According to these narratives, the pious son, Alaeddin, did not like the effect Shams had on his father and the marriage to Kimya Hatun made him even angrier. Aflaki gives an extensive narrative of this enmity, but it is doubtful whether it is reliable. On the other hand, we need to note that the reprimands of Shams in his *Maqalat* regarding Alaeddin verify the existence of a disagreement between the two. It is understood from *Ibtidaname* that Shams shared some of his secrets with Sultan Walad before his final departure. According to this, he complained to Sultan Walad about those who wanted to separate him from Rumi and said that this time no one would find him after he disappeared. His second disappearance, in 1247, still remains an unsolved mystery. According to Aflaki, Shams was slain. He narrates that when Shams was talking with Rumi, a group of seven men came near the room. One of them called Shams outside. Before leaving, Shams said to Rumi, "They are calling me to kill me," and he let out a loud scream outside and disappeared. The ones who rushed forward found nothing but a few drops of blood. Aflaki claims Rumi's son Alaeddin to be among the assassins. Aflaki again narrates that the corpse was thrown into a well, but that Sultan Walad saw it in his dream and had the body taken out, then buried near the *madrasa* of Gawhartash. However, Sultan Walad's narration casts doubt on the reliability of Aflaki's narration. For Sultan Walad reports that Shams had said, "This time, I will go away in such a way that nobody will know where I am. They will say, 'probably someone killed Shams.'" Rumi must have heard about this theory regarding murder. In some poems, he complains about such rumors:

> *Who said that the eternally alive one has died?*
> *Who said that the sun of hope has died?*
> *The enemy of that sun came on the roof,*
> *He closed his eyes, and he said that the sun is dead.*

The fact that Rumi started to search for Shams everywhere, even to the extent of going to Damascus four times himself, indicates that he did not believe—or did not want to believe— in the possibility of a murder. According to Golpinarli, the details, like the reported screams of Shams, as well as the few drops of blood on the ground, are imaginary components which appeared as the result of some mystic thought. Furuzanfar, who prepared a comprehensive monograph on Rumi, shares this opinion.

Rumi was shaken by this second loss of Shams. His friend was nowhere to be found; so he wrapped a cloud-colored turban on his head to express his mourning, and he wore it until the end of his life. Rumi, who seemingly did not have much interest in poetry before Shams, now expressed the fire in his heart through poetry and sought consolation in the *sama*, which he continued day and night. This period of turbulence and hope lasted a long time, and Rumi was ready to fall upon every piece of news about Shams. The following narration is meaningful in terms of showing this mood. One day, a man came to Rumi and said that he had seen Shams in Damascus. Rumi sprang to his feet in joy and presented the garment he was wearing to the man for bringing such good news. Another said, "He is just a liar; he did not see Shams." Upon this remark, Rumi said: "I gave all this for the false news he brought. Had it been true, I would have given him my life!"

Once, Rumi went to Damascus and sought Shams on the streets, house by house. The following couplet reflects his feelings:

How long do I have to look for you knocking on doors, one-by-one?
How long will you keep fleeing from me, from corner to corner, street to street?

After looking for Shams for nearly two years, Rumi finally accepted the new situation. Actually, the spirituality of Shams had been manifested in Rumi and he virtually became a "new Shams." In *Ibtidaname*, Sultan Walad expresses this in his father's words:

Even if we are physically apart, we are a single light without body and soul!
O you seeker! It's the same whether you saw him or me; for I am him and
he is me.
Then, if I am him, why should I look for him? I am the same as him, so
now let me talk about myself.
Like sherbet boiling in a pot, I am actually looking for myself.
Sherbet does not boil for another—it strives for its own beauty.

In another poem, he both tells about this union and reaching the true inner self through it:

I saw you as an eternal and inclusive mirror—
In your eye, I watched my own pattern and true image.
In the end, I said to myself: I have set out on a blessed journey in his eyes,
and finally I have found myself.
My image, reflected in your eyes, called out thus:
"I have become you, and you have become me. There is no separation
between us now."

Rumi also said:

Night and day, it is you who lives in my heart—
When I wish to see you, I just look into my heart.

After Shams

It can be said that the separation from Shams was a step Rumi needed to climb on the way to perfection, since the true aim was not Shams, but rather the divine light manifested in him. That light first shone within the face of Shams and caught the look of the seeker of divine love. But that face had to disappear so that it would be evident that the light did not belong essentially to that face, and then the glance would turn to the True Source. This situation was expressed in the *Masnawi* through the story of Layla and Majnun[3]. The real aim is the wine that the goblet holds, not the goblet itself. It is absolute beauty, not Layla herself. In the story, Layla is just a goblet that allows Majnun to taste the wine of love. However, Rumi does not approve of the glance being directed strictly to the human face, or the goblet, ignoring the true aim. Otherwise, that goblet or face might become an idol blocking the way to truth. In a poem, he warns that one should not become enraptured with the goblet and become too drunk with the love of the goblet—and that if one cannot turn their love toward the Creator, but rather is in love with physical beauty, then this is no different than idolatry. Then he counsels everyone not to lose time with the goblets of physicality, but rather to move on—in other words, to keep in mind that while the wine is in the goblet, the wine and goblet are not one and the same. For this reason, Rumi's eyes, ever-seeking, found new faces to reflect the divine beauty after Shams, as he found new spiritual masters. On the other hand, Rumi was not the founder of a Sufi order in the usual understanding. His restless ecstasy prevented him from taking regular care of his enthusiastic initiates. Therefore, instead of seeing him as the founder of the Mevlevi order, we can rather see him as a source of inspiration for the Mevlevi order. During the 23 years during which Rumi lived after Shams, he gave the responsibility of taking care of the new initiates to his older disciples. The first one among them was Salahaddin Zarqubi. After his death, the chief of the Ahi group, Husameddin Chelebi, carried out the same duty. Now let us take a closer look at Salahaddin.

Salahaddin was a jeweler in Konya, and he was not educated. One day, he was listening to Rumi's sermon. He was so moved that he stood up crying, went near Rumi, and put his head on his feet. Rumi liked him, too, and made him his confidant—so much so that he was one of the two fortunate people who could enter the room during Rumi's conversations with Shams. After losing Shams for good, Salahaddin became Rumi's dearest friend. Rumi found the light of Shams in Salahaddin and made him his caliph (successor). This time, we can see the same jealousy that was shown toward Shams directed toward Salahaddin. The disciples were surprised: what did Rumi find in this ignorant merchant? Why did he praise this man so much, and tell his disciples to obey him? Let us summarize this with a quote from *Ibtidanama*:

"We got rid of one, but now there is another, even worse. The previous was a light, but this one is a sparkle. Shams was a man worthy of being listened to. He would explain a subject well, and he was virtuous and learned. He was from Tabriz, and he was well-mannered, unlike this one from Konya, who is rude and unmannered. Is this the man to lead us and show the way? He is not even able to speak a couple of coherent sentences, and he can't even recite *sura Fatiha*[4] properly. What—a matchless scholar like Rumi is devoted to such an ignorant man? This jeweler Salahaddin used to sit near the entrance where we put our shoes. How can he now be given the seat of honor, and we are to call him "sheikh?" (Sultan Walad, 88)

The sources relate concrete examples of these criticisms. It is understood from them that Salahaddin could not pronounce certain words properly. For instance, he pronounced the word "*qifl*" (lock) as "qilf" and "*mubtala*" (addict) as "muftala." However, the narrations reveal that Rumi welcomed even these mistakes. Once, Salahaddin pronounced the word "*khum*" (clay pot) as "khunb," and one of those present corrected him. Rumi then said: "I know that the correct word should be '*khum*,' but given that he always says 'khunb,' I prefer his mistake over the correct pronunciation of others." (Şefik Can, 65) By acting like this, Rumi gave the message that the beloved one is loved in all aspects. Another example from the *Masnawi* expresses this very well: One day, a friend of Majnun found him patting a dog. He listed the negative attributes of the dog, and he protested to Majnun about what he was doing. Majnun replied: "This dog guards the neighborhood where Layla lives. I wouldn't exchange a single hair of such a dog in return for so many lions." (*Masnawi*, 3:22)

As narrated by Sultan Walad, the reactions reached such a degree that some jealous disciples thought of murdering Salahaddin, but they could not find sufficient courage to do so. (Sultan Walad, 92)

Some narrations in the sources give an idea of Salahaddin's sincere heart, which is perhaps why he deserved such love. Here is one of them. One day, Rumi happened to pass near the jewelry shops. When he heard the hammers banging on gold, he was enraptured and started whirling. Salahaddin motioned his workers to keep hammering, ran to his master, and stooped at his feet. The whirling lasted until the gold had turned to dust. Rumi admired Saladdin's purity of heart. He expressed his feelings thus:

> *The one who comes is not a jeweler but the treasure itself,*
> *What a character! What an appearance! What a beauty! What a beauty!*

The fact that there are 71 poems by Rumi in praise of Salahaddin indicates how much Rumi loved him. However, Rumi did not stop at this, and he arranged for his son, Sultan Walad, to marry Salahaddin Zarqubi's daughter Fatma Hatun; thereby adding a bond of kinship to the bond of the heart. A paragon of virtue in every way, Rumi made an affectionate father-in-law to his new daughter. He taught her how to read and write, including how to read the Qur'an. At that time, the couple was experiencing problems, and Rumi warned his son to be kind to his wife. He cared for his relatives in every way. For instance, he also helped Salahaddin's other daughter, Hadiya Hatun, to marry. And he asked Gurju Hatun, the wife of his disciple, Parwana, to support Hadiya Hatun in regards to the dowry. Gurju Hatun sent so many things that they could not find enough room to place them, and some of them had to be left to Fatma Hatun. (Önder, 126)

In comparison to the boisterous Shams, Salahaddin was a reserved person who spoke little, and he was very sensitive in following the principles of Islam. After serving Rumi for ten years, he passed away in December of 1258 CE. As an example of his piety, he had a bath every Friday morning, even in winter. Although his robe was still wet after being washed, he would put it on, for he did not want to abandon a tradition of the Prophet. He answered those who warned him about becoming ill by saying, "Pleasing God is more important than my health." (Furuzanfar, 138)

On the other hand, we understand from his will that he saw death as if it were a wedding, like his master, Rumi. In conformance with his will, his funeral was accompanied by the *sama* and hymns. (Sultan Walad, 142)

Rumi, who favored spiritual maturity over knowledge, despite being a scholar, chose Husameddin Chelebi, of Konya, to substitute Salahaddin. The family of Husameddin had immigrated to Konya from Urmiya. Husameddin was born in 1225 in Konya. On the death of his father at a young age, Husameddin had become the leader of the Ahi group, a brotherhood of small tradesmen. Later on, he was dedicated to Rumi with all the members of his group, and he became famous for his loyalty to Rumi—to the extent that Rumi sent all the gifts he received to his loyal disciple, and he entrusted all his affairs to Husameddin. Previously, we mentioned an example from the *Masnawi* about *Majnun*, who loved even the dog that guarded the street where Layla lived. This summarizes Rumi's feelings for Husameddin. One day, when Rumi and his friends were going to visit Husameddin Chelebi, they came across a dog at the beginning of the street. One of them wanted to chase it away, but Rumi prevented him and said: "Do not touch it. It is not an ordinary dog, for it inhabits Husameddin's neighborhood! (Önder, 144)

Sultan Walad narrates that his father likened Shams to the sun, Salahaddin to the moon, and Husameddin to a star (Sultan Walad, 143). In this comparison, even if Husameddin falls behind Salahaddin, the service he provided is certainly far greater, because the *Masnawi* actually appeared at the request of Husameddin. During a conversation, he petitioned Rumi to write a text which would be a guidebook for dervishes, like Attar's *Mantiqut Tayr,* or

Sanai's *Ilahinama*. On hearing this, Rumi produced a page from his turban. It was the first story of his *Masnawi*, the first 18 couplets known as "The Song of the Reed." The lines, which strike us with their beauty, are apparently the story of an ordinary reed turning into a flute and making fascinating sounds. In reality, it is nothing but the story of a man and his aim of being in the world. A good flute is the best master for reeds; it can show them how to become a flute. The flute was Rumi himself. He had a gradual experience with fire: he, too, had been burned and purified like the reed—and in the end there was nothing left inside him in terms of ego. His burned body was like a reed-flute, voicing the breath of its owner, whispering the secrets of eternity to intent ears:

THE SONG OF THE REED

Listen to this reed-flute, how it is wistfully singing!
About separation, it is complaining:

"Ever since I was uprooted from the reed-bed,
All eyes gazing upon my cry shed tears that never dried.

"I want a bosom torn, torn from separation,
So that I may share the pain of lamentation:

"Whoever has been parted from his origin
Always yearns for the moment of reunion.

"In every company, I moaned and cried,
The miserable and the happy, both in friendship tried.

"Each became friendly with me according to their fancy,
Yet none sought to discover the secrets deep within me.

"Though my secret is in the notes I wail,
The senses are unable to unveil,

"Body from soul, and soul from body are not concealed,
Yet to no mortal eye is the soul ever revealed."

'Tis the fervor of love in the reed's wailing breath; not mere hot air,
May he be naught if he be lacking this fervent desire for fire.

It's the flame of love in this reed-flute that burns,
It's the ferment of love in this wine that enraptures.

The reed-flute is the confidant of all who are parted from the beloved,
Its wailing tones shred the shrouds of hearts deeply covered.

Who has seen one like the reed-flute in grief, yet with a cure in its pain?
Who has seen one like the reed-flute—a longing lover and a true companion?

The reed-flute sings of the way stained with blood
It tells of the beloved for whom Majnun's heart bled.

None but the crazed lover can truly say something to be heard,
For the wise tongue carries away only the lowly ear.

Reunion is held up as the days grow, lengthening,
Nights pull together with blazing suffering.

Who cares for painful days now gone?
For You remain, O You Pure One!

Only the fish drowning in water grow thirstier,
Yet the days of those with no share grow longer.

This reed's ecstatic state of love, to the mature, is all-comprehensible,
But beyond the grasp of the raw, to whom my only word is, "Farewell!"

These lines were the beginning of an oral and written style which was, and is, unique in history. As Rumi himself says, the blessing of milk is not to be ascribed to the udder, but to the hand that milks it. Husameddin's hand, i.e. his request, activated the unending seas of inspiration in Rumi, and he wrote down the words that poured out of him. There was no special time allocated for this. He could be anywhere—in the market, at home, on the street, or at night until the morning. Actually, while the poems in Rumi's divan were also written down by others, the entire *Masnawi* was written down by Husameddin Chelebi himself. He was rapidly taking notes as Rumi spoke, and later on read it aloud to his master for correction. For his part, Rumi genuinely appreciated the efforts of his loyal disciple. In many parts of the *Masnawi,* and particularly in the prefaces found in each volume, he praised Husameddin heartily and noted that the work had been written thanks to him. The two-year interval between the first two volumes actually verifies this point. When the first volume of the *Masnawi* was finished, Husameddin Chelebi lost his wife, and this shook him very much. He retired into himself and put aside pen and paper. When the hand of demand did not milk the source of inspiration, the flow came to a halt. Only after Husameddin was able to bring himself out of his mourning did Rumi continue the *Masnawi* from where he had left off. What Rumi says in *Fihi Mafih* about the significance of the listener can be summarized as follows:

"Our words are like the water controlled by a gate-keeper. When the gate-keeper opens the gate, the water doesn't know where to flow. What I know is that if the water flows abundantly, there is much parched land to be watered. If the water is little, then there much land cannot be watered. Likewise, in a *hadith*,[5] it is stated that God gives a good command of speech to a speaker in conformance with the eagerness of the listeners. I am just a shoemaker. I have plenty of leather, but I adjust the shoes according to the size of the foot. I have plenty of cloth, but I'm a tailor who makes a suit according to the body." (*Fihi Mafih*, 162).

The Final Journey

During the ten-year period when Husameddin Chelebi was sheikh, Rumi led a relatively quiet life and spent his time writing and counseling. Toward the end of 1273, Rumi caught a serious illness, and the doctors could not bring his high fever down. They were unable to find a cause—but Rumi was simply world-weary. As the doctors realized this, they increasingly lost hope, and the people of Konya waited in anxiety. On the other hand, Rumi was content and cheerful. He answered Sadeddin Konevi, who wished him good health, saying "May cure and good health be yours—now there is a veil as thin as a hair between the lover and the beloved." Then he uttered the following couplet:

I have taken off the body, that work of imagination.
Now I sway on, enjoying the pleasure of reunion. (Masnawi, 6:4619)

Here is another of his couplets about death:

Given that it is You who takes life, dying is so sweet.
As long as I am with You, death is sweeter than life indeed. (Şefik Can, 92)

He would protest to those who wished for him to live longer. When his wife said, "I wish you were to live for 400 years so that you could fill the world with the light of reality," he replied, "Am I the Pharaoh, or Nimrod, that I would wish for such a long life? I did not come to the prison called "the world" to stay for so long. I am looking forward to joining the company of the Prophet."

His faithful son, Sultan Walad, did not leave his bedside even for an instant, but even he could not bear to see his father in this condition. The last words of Rumi were a consolation for the son, and he left this world giving new meaning to death. People learned from Rumi's death that dying is not a separation but a reunion, not sadness but joy, not vinegar but sweet sherbet. From then on, many called death "the night of reunion."[6]

Before dying, he dictated his will, and of the advice that he left behind, the following words were included: "I wish you to fear God wherever you are, to eat little, sleep little, speak little, refrain from committing evil, keep up your prayers and fasting, and put up with misbehavior from people. The best of people is the one who does good to them, and the best talk is little and concise. And all praise belongs to God." (Furuzanfar, 152)

The news of his death sent a shockwave through Konya. Young and old, everybody rushed to the funeral. People of the city, villagers, children, and adults; Christians, Jews, and Muslims—everybody was there. The followers of the three Abrahamic religions in Konya all mourned. And the coffin which was carried through a great crowd could only make its way to its standing stone for the prayer towards evening. At the funeral sermon, the spirit of Rumi was addressing the crowd, saying:

"On the day I die, when you see my coffin being carried, don't think that I care for this world. Do not cry or feel woe for me, for it is the very day of my reunion. When you bury the body, don't be sad about separation—for this is the time when I shall meet the Beloved, my reunion. You have seen me set, haven't you? Then you must also see the rise, then. Are the sun and the moon harmed when they set? You think I am buried under the ground, don't you? But I have the seven firmaments under my feet." (Furuzanfar, 156)

Sheikh Sadreddin Konevi, who stepped forward to lead the funeral prayer, could bear it no longer and he fainted. Upon this event, Qadi Sirajeddin replaced him, and they buried Rumi's feather-light body next to that of his father. Before long, some of the rich men in Konya came together, and they had a beautiful tomb built around his grave. However, Rumi had found a far better place than a tomb to reside, as he himself had said:

> When we die, don't seek our graves under the ground.
> You can find us in the hearts that love.

His Appearance

As related by Furuzanfar and other sources, Rumi was thin and tall. He had a pale complexion, grey beard, dark eyebrows, and hazel eyes. One day, when he saw his body in a public bath in the mirror he felt ashamed because of the sufferings he had made it bear. His pale complexion is also alluded to in many of his poems. His being underweight is thought to be the result of the abstention he went through in his youth and the long fasts he observed. Aflaki relates that he ate once in three days, sometimes once a week, and that he took long retreats for worship. (Aflaki, I: 444,501) We have already mentioned that Sayyid Burhaneddin put him into *chila* three consecutive times.[7] However, it is understood that Rumi abandoned strict austerity after meeting Shams and advised his disciples to do so. Likewise, when his son Sultan Walad was twenty, he asked his father's permission to perform *chila* and Rumi answered as follows:

"There is no *chila* in our way. It is found in the ways of Moses and Jesus." He averted his disciples from *chila*. Instead, he wished them to be involved in social life, but not to attach their hearts to worldly affairs (Furuzanfar, 98). The following couplet summarizes this idea:

> *Worldliness is being oblivious to God,*
> *It is not having wealth, clothes, children, or a wife.*

Rumi had an awe-inspiring face; and his eyes—the mirror of his soul—were keen, reflecting his attraction toward God. Nobody could fix their gaze into his eyes, and they would simply look elsewhere.

At the beginning, he wore a scholar's turban and a new loose robe. After meeting Shams, he started wearing the light-blue dervish mantle called *faraja*, and an ash-gray turban. (Furuzanfar, 190, 191)

His Inner World and Ethical Conduct

The Prophet is said to have had a character that perfectly reflected Qur'anic ethics. Rumi modeled himself after the Prophet of Islam, and the sources that shaped his ethical conduct were the Qur'an and the Sunna. Nowadays, there is a popular trend to present Rumi in a surreligious position. Rumi virtually gave a reply to this accusation centuries ago, by emphasizing his attachment to the Messenger of God and how disturbed he felt at such a twisting of the facts:

> *I'm a slave of the Qur'an as long as I live,*
> *And I am the soil of the way of Muhammad, the chosen one.*
> *If anyone reports my words otherwise,*
> *I will complain about those words and their owner.*

Undoubtedly, Rumi had a rather abundant tolerance which cannot be found in every Sufi. However, he frames the limits of this tolerance as follows:

> *Like a pair of compasses, I put one foot on the Sharia firmly,*
> *While my other foot travels to all seventy-two nations.*

Thus, Rumi reveals the source of his exemplary and admirable morals. When he talks about the Prophet in *Fihi Mafih*, he likens him to the sun, and all the rest of the people who receive their light from him to candles. Consequently, the source of the light and beauty of the candles is the sun.

Rumi was educated under the supervision of his father. After he completed his studies, he made spiritual progress under the guidance of Shams. Consequently, he was purified from his ego and he became a person who only saw harmony and beauty when he looked at the universe. Here is a couplet summarizing this view:

> The major fault is seeing nothing but faulty things,
> Can the souls traveling to the realms beyond see any faults?

His lofty level of perception comprehended the harmony in the universe which reveals only a little as the visible realm; he recognized the concordance beyond these seeming opposites. The universe deserved love and respect in terms of being a home that had been divinely granted, as did the creation and its inhabitants. This was such a profound understanding that he was even was able to say, "one who reaches the world of no colors can see there Moses and the Pharaoh in peace." (*Masnawi*, vol. I, 2467)

In effect, divine manifestations have no color; they stream on in different shapes and appearances at every instant. Rumi, who had reached that realm, kept being in different states and appearances as well. One of his followers, Gurju Hatun, wished to have Rumi's portrait drawn as a souvenir, as her husband had been appointed to a position in Kayseri. She commissioned an artist, Aynuddevlevi, for this. Rumi stood and smiled, saying, "Come and draw it if you can."

The artist painted the first portrait and looked up. He was astonished to see a different face from that which he had drawn. He made another portrait from the start, and then he looked up to see Rumi looking different once again. This lasted for some time, and the poor artist put down his brush in the end. Rumi expressed this with the following words: "I am colorless and indefinite. Even I cannot see myself as I am—so how can *you*?" (Önder, 154)

Human beings are one of the manifestations created by God, fixed in a shape. Colors, forms, and habits can only be pinpointed in frozen objects. However, a mirror does not have its own shape, and the sights in the mirror are in a state of perpetual change. Likewise, Rumi is as formless as a mirror before divine manifestations. Therefore, he represents an all-welcoming understanding, independent of color, language, or country; in effect, he appeals to all people and he reflects what all hearts yearn for. In this respect, we can say that in the famous parable of four men buying grapes,[8] the traveler who realizes their shared aim and helps them denotes Rumi himself. So Rumi was full of a God-oriented love, understanding, and affection toward all creatures with such a mindset. Now, let us relate some examples reflecting this perspective of Rumi's: As narrated in Molla Jami's, *Nafahatul Uns*, Sirajeddin of Konya protested about Rumi saying, "I am together with all 72 nations." He sent one of his friends to Rumi to speak about it. The man asked Rumi whether he had really said such a thing, with the intention of disgracing him in public. When Rumi answered in the affirmative, the man started sputtering curses at him. Rumi smiled back and said: "In spite of all you say, I am together with you as well." (Furuzanfar, 193) He formulated his approach simply as, "We have come to this world not to divide, but to unite." He couldn't stand seeing fights and rivalries. One day, he saw two men fighting. One of them was threatening the other thus: "You just tell me one, and I will reply with a thousand more." Rumi told him: "Whatever you will say, say it to me. Even if you say a thousand things, you will not hear anything in return." (Önder, 176) He was well aware that fire cannot be extinguished by fire. The fire of rage and grudge can only be put out by the water of affection. One day, he gave his son, Sultan Walad, the following golden advice on friendship: "If you want to love your enemy and be loved by him, wish goodness for him for forty days. In the end, you will see that he will become your closest friend, for there are ways from one heart to another." (Önder, 177)

Rumi had smashed his ego onto the ground, like shattered glass, and his modesty was peerless. Owing to the respect he felt for God's works, he would not discriminate between people. He treated people equally, as if there were no differences of religion, ethnicity, or status between them. One day, when he heard his daughter, Malika Hatun, telling off her maidservant, he felt very sorry and uttered the following words of wisdom: "Why are you hurting her? What would you do if she were the lady and you were the maid? Do you wish me to issue a *fatwa* and declare that no one has any servants but God! In truth, all of them are our sisters and fellow citizens." (Yeniterzi, 21)

As Aflaki narrates, some people criticized the fact that Rumi's disciples were lower-class people. They said, "We have nothing to say about Rumi himself, but his disciples are commoners, like grocers, tailors, and so on. None of those around Rumi are mature or qualified people." Rumi simply replied as follows: "Had they been qualified people, I would be their disciple. I accepted them as my disciples since they are not qualified." (Furuzanfar, 195)

Rumi did not approve of laziness and encouraged those around him to be industrious. He would say, "We have forbidden our disciples from begging." He would not accept alms, and he lived on the money he received in return for the *fatwa*s he issued. According to the translation of Nafahat, he would be glad when there was nothing at his home and say: "Thanks God, our home is like those of the prophets' today." He would neither be obliged to anyone, nor would he make anyone obliged to him. For this reason, he would give away the presents sent to him, but he did not want this to be known by the people so as not to show off. From time to time, he secretly put money in the pockets of each of his students at the *madrasa*. Once, he wished to give money to Osman Guyende, one of his poor students, but he did not want to embarrass him before the others. He said "O, Osman! You used to have a beautiful habit of shaking hands with me. What's happened to you that you have given it up?" While shaking hands, he put the money in his palm to him and said, "From now on, do not forget to come and shake my hand often." (Yeniterzi, 26)

Rumi did not like to be favored over others. Once when he went to the public bath, there were lepers inside. The keeper demanded that they leave the pool immediately, but Rumi stopped him. As was the custom, he wrapped a long towel around his waist, and he took a bath with the lepers. Likewise, he would not consent to anyone being told to get up for him; he would just walk away to prevent this. (Furuzanfar, 196)

Rumi knew how to be a beloved spouse, an affectionate father, an understanding father-in-law, and a sweet grandfather. Among his children, he loved Sultan Walad the most, and he said to him, "You are the one who takes after me the most. My coming to this world was for the sake of your coming." Also, when his grandson, Amir Arif Chelebi, was born in 1272, he could not contain his excitement, and he started whirling in ecstasy. (Önder, 195-6)

The following anecdote reveals both his humorous nature and his attitude against superstitions. One day, his wife, Kira Hatun, was sewing on a loose button. Due to the superstition which claims, "It is inauspicious to sew a button on while the owner is wearing the garment," she asked Rumi to put a straw in his mouth to avert the purported harm. Rumi smiled and said: "Don't be afraid. There is the *Sura Ikhlas*[9] from the Qur'an in my mouth. I hold it so tight that nothing can happen to me." (Önder, 188)

Animals also received their share of Rumi's compassion, too, as was the case with God's Messenger himself. There was a dog with her puppies near a ruined wall. She could not leave them to find food and they were hungry. Drawing from his compassion, Rumi fed the dogs for several days. (Önder, 195)

Although he was a matchless scholar, he took no pride in this accomplishment. On the contrary, when he proved his argument, he behaved as if he had lost, even in his youth. He appreciated being faithful in friendship, and when he took an oath, he would say, "For the sake of the faithfulness of the chivalrous." In short, in his time, Rumi was the most successful person to model themselves on Prophet Muhammad's exemplary ethics.

Rumi's Environment in Konya

Let us take a look at the socio-political situation of the period and become acquainted with the officials and friends of Rumi. Baha Walad had come to Konya during the reign of the powerful sultan, Alaeddin Kaykubat. However, at the time of Rumi, this state was in decline. On the death of Alaeddin Kaykubat, in 1237, Giyaseddin Kayhusrav, who was not as competent a leader as his father, ascended to the throne. In 1242, after a Mongolian army of 30,000, commanded by Baiju, demolished Erzurum, Kayhusrav pursued them with his own army. The Battle of Kosedag, which followed that event, was a total defeat for the Seljuks, and it brought the end of the state. Thus, Anatolia came under Mongolian control. In 1256, the Seljuks had a second try, but they lost again. The Mongols crowned Giyaseddin Kayhusrav's son, Rukneddin Kilicarslan IV, who was in prison. However, the real power was held by Muineddin Suleyman, the head of the land registry office, who was also known as Muineddin Parwana. When the Mongols left, after staying in the vicinity of Konya for a many years, the sultan wanted to put an end to Parwana's power. However, Parwana, who had made an agreement with the Mongols, gained the advantage in the struggle, and he had the sultan killed. Then the late sultan's son, Giyaseddin Kayhusrav III, who was only two and a half years old, was declared the new sultan. Muineddin Parwana, who was still the actual ruler of the state, was himself killed by the Mongols in 1277. In the aftermath, battles for the throne continued until the end of the Seljuk State, in 1308.

In such a chaotic era, Rumi became a source of hope and energy for society, contributing his works and ideas. He embraced all classes of society, and his door was open to everyone. Along with common citizens, people from the royal court also found spiritual support in Rumi, and they showed him due respect. Rumi, on the other hand, did not go beyond counseling them, and he refused to interfere in politics. He always kept his dignified position in his relationship with the administrators.

Two sultans, Izzeddin Kaykavus II (reign 1245-57) and
Rukneddin Kilicarslan IV (reign 1257-66) were among those who
attended his talks. Aflaki narrates that Sultan Izzeddin Kaykavus was
skeptical about the spiritual greatness of Rumi at the beginning.
With the encouragement of his vizier, Sahip Shamseddin, an admirer of Rumi, the sultan consented to attend a sermon. After listening
to him, the sultan changed his mind completely and became a disciple of Rumi. On the other hand, his brother, Rukneddin, was a fol-
lower of Rumi at the start, later on became inclined toward Sheikh
Baba of Merent and started to call him "father." It is narrated that
Rumi was heartbroken on learning this, and he pronounced the following: "If you found a new 'father,' then we will find a new 'son.'"
(Aflaki, 1:204) Aflaki sees the slaying of Sultan Rukneddin as a misfortune which befell him because he forsook Rumi. The poem which
begins with the following lines in *Divani Kabir* is thought to express
the sorrow Rumi felt after the incident:

> *I told you not to go there—they might inflict a calamity on you…*
> (Aflaki, I:205)

The prominent figures of the time—Sahip Shamseddin,
Jalaladdin Karatay, Tajeddin Mutez, and Muineddin Parwana—were
also followers of Rumi. Parwana was a very clever person who kept
a balanced policy in his relations with the Mongols and ruled the
state for years. However, even he couldn't be saved from being
killed by Abaka Khan, in 1277 CE, for having cooperated with the
Egyptian sultan, Baibars, against the Mongols.

During his reign, Parwana often donated money for sacrificial
animals and sent presents as charity, along with building facilities for
the public. Rumi, who acted as an intermediary for the poor, men-
tions his name frequently in *Fihi Mafih*. However, except for the
times when he had to, Rumi did not like to meet important people,
as he preferred spending his time with the poor instead.
(Furuzanfar, 182-89)

In addition to the people mentioned above, the following
names can be counted among those who were devoted to Rumi:

Qadi Izzeddin, of Konya; Amir Badreddin Gevhertas; Majduddin Atabeg; Aminuddin Mikail; Sahip Fakhreddin; Alemuddin Kayser; Jalaladdin Mustavfi; Atabeg Arslandogmus; Kirsehir's Judge, Jajaoglu Nureddin; and Rumi's own doctor, Akmaladdin al-Nahjevani. There were also notable women, like Muinuddin Parwana's wife, Gurju Hatun, and Kilicarslan IV's wife, Gumach Hatun, among his followers.

Owing to some of his expressions, there were claims that Rumi held pro-Mongolian views. However, when his remarks about the Mongols are taken as a whole, it will be seen that these are false claims. In several statements, Rumi directly or indirectly condemns the Mongol oppression, and he expresses the opinion that their power couldn't last long. In addition, he criticizes their traditions, like that of shooting arrows to the sky near a dying person with the hope of driving away the angel of death. As for his remarks which underline the idea that one needs to be afraid of one's own carnal-self rather than the Mongols, these should be taken within the context of Sufism. Also, his prediction that the Mongols would accept Islam was realized in time. Due to the Mongolian invasion, the 13th century became a period of disaster politically. On the other hand, Islamic thought was maintained, and there were still great thinkers and Sufis being educated. Along with the statesmen of the time, Rumi met many famous scholars and spiritual masters as well; the degree of his friendship with these people varied. The following names can be counted among them:

Muhyiddin Ibn Arabi (d. 1241): His works *Fusus al-Hikam* and *Futuhat al-Makkiya* are among the classics of Sufi literature. Ibn Arabi is probably the only great Sufi master to be compared with Rumi in terms of his novel perspectives and the influence he had. Among the Sufis, Rumi was a representative of love to an extreme. Relatively speaking, Ibn Arabi had a more systematic nature, and his more tolerant attitude toward philosophers, in comparison to Rumi, supports this fact.

These two famous Sufi masters—one of whom was the voice of love and the other of logic—flowed on in their own beds like

two great rivers, producing lasting effects on the world of Islam
through the followers they left behind. According to W. Chittick,
commentators on the *Masnawi* from the following generation
ignored the differences in their individual natures and took as their
basis Ibn Arabi's ideas, for he presents a ready-made system.
(Chittick, 718) Yet, although they lived in the same century, a comparison of their works actually presents little similarity, which indicates that they were not much influenced by one another. In fact,
in commenting on what he learned from Rumi, Shams addressed
Ibn Arabi thus: "I benefited from him very much—but incompa-
rable to the benefit I had from you. How can we compare pearls to
pebbles?" (Golpinarli, 52) It is understood from this statement that
when Shams was in Damascus, he spent quite a long time near Ibn
Arabi, but he did not like him much. Likewise, some words of
Shams in *Maqalat* prove that, from time-to-time, he argued with
Ibn Arabi and criticized him (Golpinarli, 52-3) Also, during his
education in Damascus, Rumi must have met this great Sufi, as he
was still alive at that time. The fact that Ibn Arabi uses a couplet
taken from of Rumi's *Divani Kabir* (5:2127) while telling about
divine love in *Fusus al-Hikam* supports this:

> I have become a lover and all people realized this,
> But they did not understand who is the One I love.

On the other hand, except for the natural parallel in terms of
Sufi mentality, no influence of Ibn Arabi's system on Rumi can be
detected. His close friend, Sadreddin Konevi, must have been the
channel through which Rumi became familiar with the ideas of Ibn
Arabi. (Şefik Can, 337-43)

Sadreddin Konevi (d.1274): Sadreddin Konevi was the
adopted son and successor of Ibn Arabi. He held a key role in correctly interpreting Ibn Arabi's difficult ideas in a context compatible with Islamic faith. A leading scholar of his time in the study of
hadith, he had both a *madrasa* and a dervish lodge in Konya. At the
beginning, he was skeptical about Rumi, but later on became one
of his admirers. His comparison of Rumi with two masters who
lived in the past indicates how much he valued Rumi: "Were

Junayd al-Baghdadi and Bayezid al-Bistami alive today, they would hold on to Rumi's saddle flap." Rumi's choice of Sadreddin to lead his funeral prayer also indicates his love for him.

Qutbeddin Mahmud of Shiraz (d. 1310): He was originally from Kazerun, and he was one of the outstanding representatives of Ibn Sina's school of medicine. Also, he had learned astronomical observation and mathematics from Hodja Nasiruddin Tusi. Later, he became the Chief Judge of Sivas. Aflaki narrates that Qutbeddin Mahmud met Rumi in Konya and became one of his disciples.

Fakhreddin Iraqi (d.1289): He was originally from Hemedan. He studied *Fusus al-Hikam* and *Futuhat al-Makkiya* with his teacher, Sadreddin Konevi, and he wrote *Lamaat* with the inspiration he received from them. According to Aflaki, from time-to-time he would join the *sama* with Rumi and become enraptured. When his protector, Parwana, was killed, Fakhreddin Iraqi went to Egypt, then to Damascus, and there he died.

Najmeddin Razi (d.1256): Najmeddin Razi, who was commonly known as "Daya," was from the city of Rey. He was the successor of the great sheikh, Najmeddin Kubra. After fleeing the Mongols and coming to Konya, he was welcomed by Sultan Alaeddin Kaykubat. Together with Sadreddin, he sometimes attended Rumi's circles as well.

Bahaeddin Kani (d. approx. 1273): He is mainly famous for two works, *Seljuknama*, a history of the Seljuks, as well as a translation of *Kalila wa Dimna* in verse. It is understood that he was not an open-minded person. Once, when he was near Rumi with his friends, he criticized Sanai for the way he used his own verses along with Qur'anic verses, and he said that he did not even consider Sanai to be a Muslim. On hearing this, Rumi became angry and rebuked him: "You don't consider Sanai a Muslim? If you saw what a Muslim he is, you would be so baffled that your cap would fly off! Do you mean that he is not a Muslim but *you* are?" Still, Kani's poems reveal how much he loved Rumi.

Sirajaddin of Urmiya (d. 1283 CE): He was among the most renowned scholars of the time. Sirajaddin wrote a famous book on logic entitled *Matail al-Anwar*. Sirajeddin spent his final years in Konya. At the beginning, he was opposed to Rumi, but later on, he acknowledged the latter's greatness.

Safiyyeddin of India (d. 1315 CE): He completed his education in Konya and later became the judge of Damascus. It is understood from the words of Rumi that he did not have a very positive opinion of Safiyyeddin, a man proud of his knowledge: "Purifying the heart of Safiyeddin is more difficult than converting 70 idolators to Islam, for his soul is blackened like a blackboard for children." But later on, Rumi agreed to accept him as a disciple upon the request of Sultan Walad.

Sheikh Sadi of Shiraz (d. 1292): Sheikh Sadi was a famous poet in his field, with his texts, *Gulistan* and *Bostan*. He came to Anatolia a few times and he probably met Rumi as well. Aflaki narrates that when a sovereign named Shamseddin Hindi asked for a good poem from Sheikh Sadi, he sent a couplet from Rumi in reply. Some claim that the rich but thrifty sheikh mentioned in *Gulistan* represents Rumi, but factually this does not fit. (Furuzanfar, 160-81)

In addition to these people, there were also others who met Rumi and attended his talks: Haji Mubarak Haydar, Qutbeddin of Shiraz, Humamuddin of Tabriz, and Hodja Reshiduddin can be counted among them. Again, the leading figures of Anatolian Turkish poetry, such as Yunus Emre and Haji Bektash Veli, visited Rumi as well. In particular, research reveals that Rumi had a strong influence on Yunus Emre. (Şefik Can, 355)

THE MEVLEVI ORDER AND THE SAMA

The Mevlevi Order, which took its basis from Rumi's ideas and memories, was established after his death. Thanks to Rumi's eldest son, Sultan Walad, it was institutionalized as a Sufi order. Being a good organizer, Sultan Walad opened up Mevlevi Sufi lodges not only in Konya but also in many different parts of Anatolia. The order kept expanding in the Ottoman period as well, and there were Mevlevi lodges in almost all the major cities. There were 114 Mevlevi lodges in total spread throughout Anatolia, the Balkans, and Arab lands. The foremost cities to be counted among them were Konya, Afyon, Kutahya, Manisa, Mugla, Eskisehir, Bursa, Denizli, Istanbul, Bursa, Antep, Diyarbakır, Urfa, Adana, Ankara, Yozgat, Kastamonu, Sivas, Salonica, Belgrade, Bosnia, Cairo, Mecca, Medina, Damascus, Aleppo, Tabriz, and Lefkosa.

The Mevlevi lodges were a kind of school where dervishes learned how to whirl on the *mashk* board with a nail driven right in the middle. In addition, they also served the lodge by working as street vendors or craftsmen. In fact, they were required to perform 18 different jobs to complete their 1001-day period as initiates. Along with these services, a dervish also learned arts like calligraphy, engraving, tile painting, music and the like, in accordance with their respective talents. Those who completed the 1001 days successfully were given the title "*Dada*," and a room would be allocated for them. This being the general practice, there were also dervishes who learned the *sama* and fulfilled the tradition of the order before they finished the 1001 days.

With the establishment of the Mevlevi Order, reading the *Masnawi* was also made into a discipline. The people who were responsible for reading and explaining the *Masnawi* in dervish lodges and mosques were called, "*Masnawihan*." *Masnawihan*s had to be authorized by the Chelebi in Konya, or by another *Masnawihan*. Damat Ibrahim Pasha made it obligatory in his *madrasa* that the *Masnawi* be studied. In the 19th century, *Masnawi* centers were founded for enabling those who were not Mevlevi to study the *Masnawi*.

As it is seen in both the *Masnawi* and the *Divan*, Rumi laid great importance on the *sama*. According to him, "The *sama* is the food of lovers; for in the *sama*, there is the dream of meeting with God." The following poem of Rumi's expresses how he perceived the *sama*:

> *What is Sama, do you know?*
> *It is hearing the sound of "yes,"*
> *Of separating one from oneself and reaching the Lord,*
> *Seeing and knowing the state of the Friend,*
> *And hearing, through divine veils, the secrets of the Lord.*
> *What is Sama, do you know?*
> *Being ignorant of existence and tasting eternity in the ultimate mortality.*
> *What is Sama, do you know?*
> *Struggling with the carnal soul; fluttering on the ground like a half-slain hen.*
> *What is Sama, do you know?*
> *Feeling the cure of Prophet Jacob, and sensing the arrival of Prophet Joseph from the scent of a shirt.*
> *What is Sama, do you know?*
> *Like the staff of Prophet Moses, it is swallowing all the tricks of the Pharaoh's magicians.*
> *What is Sama, do you know?*
> *Opening the heart like Shams-i Tabrizi [an excellent devotee],*
> *And seeing the Divine light.*
> (Şefik Can, 264)

As related from Sultan Walad and Sipahsalar, Rumi did not perfom the *sama* himself, or did not care much about it, before he met Shams. Although there is no definite information on when or how Rumi performed the *sama*, we know that many times he started doing the *sama* at the Sufi lodge, at home, and at the market; sometimes during his lessons; and sometimes even when he was issuing a *fatwa*—always under the effect of divine love. He performed the *sama* spontaneously, then, without any ceremonial rules. We have already mentioned how he started whirling on hearing the sound of gold being hammered in Salahaddin's jewelry shop. We learn from Aflaki Dada's narration that, including the Seljuk Royal Palace and its neighboring cities, Rumi performed the *sama* with many people in various circles. This natural and unregulated way of practicing the *sama* continued through the time of Sultan Walad and the following generations. In time, however, it became a systemized ceremony. According to Golpinarli, it was Pir

Adil Chelebi (d. 1460 CE), who was the Mevlevi Sheikh for 39 years, who gave the *sama* its final shape as it is performed today. (Golpinarli, 1963, 48)

The Symbols of the Sama

As it is practiced today, everything in the *sama*—from the garments the performers wear to the set actions—holds a symbolic meaning. Accordingly, the circular ground for the *sama* represents the universe. The red hide laid for the Sheikh is an allusion reminding witnesses of Rumi's death at sunset, and it also denotes the reunion with God. As an indication of the killing of the ego before actual death, the dervishes wear a conical felt hat representing a gravestone. With the same purpose, they wear a *tennureh*—a white suit representing a shroud. A dark robe worn over the *tennureh* represents the carnal self. Before a dervish starts the sama, he leaves this robe—the carnal self—behind and steps toward spiritual purity. The crossed arms with hands on the shoulders denote the acknowledgement of God's unity. And whirling from right to left, opening both arms sideways, symbolizes embracing the universe with one's entire heart. The right hand with the palm turned towards the heavens receives from God, and the left hand facing the ground gives away to people. The *sama* ceremony is initiated with the *Naat*, a hymn praising the Prophet, composed by Itri (d. 1712 CE). The thudding of the *Qudum*—the camel-skin drum—represents God's command "*Kun!*" (Be!) at the creation of the universe, while the sound of the *ney* represents the divine breath blown into man. After these, *samazans*—whirling dervishes—walk the *sama* ground behind the sheikh, making three tours, which is a prelude to the spiritual journey to come. After they take off the dark robe which represents their carnal self, they bow before the Sheikh to get his permission, and the *sama*, or the spiritual journeying, commences. The four greetings in the *sama* mark four different phases:

Recognition of one's position as a servant of God.

Adoration felt before His greatness.

Transformation of the admiration into divine love and the complete surrender to Him.

Return to the aim of creation—servanthood to God.

In brief, the *sama* can be summarized thus: the servant leaves behind his carnal self and annihilates his ego in God. At the end of this spiritual progress, there is a return to the duty of servanthood as a mature person in full obedience.

CHAPTER 2

HIS WORKS

R umi wrote his works in Persian, which was the prevalent language used in literature in his time. Some poems and letters that he wrote in Arabic reveal his profound command of Arabic. In addition, he has some mixed-language (*mulamma*) poems, where he also uses Turkish alongside Persian.

THE MASNAWI

Being his most renowned work, the *Masnawi* is considered among the masterpieces of Sufi literature in terms of the influence it had on both the time in which it was written and later periods. The *Masnawi* consists of six volumes. In Sultan Walad's version there are 25,668 couplets in total. Actually, the *masnawi* is a genre in classic Arab, Persian, and Turkish literature. The word "*masnawi*" means "in twos," and it denotes a work written in verse where each couplet has its own rhyme. Due to this individual rhyming system, a *masnawi* is suitable for expressing long topics without having to adhere to the same rhyme. This must be the reason why Rumi wrote his masterpiece as a *masnawi*. In time, however, the *Masnawi* became so famous that the word brought Rumi's work to mind, not the genre. The *Masnawi* commentator Ankaravi thinks that Rumi chose the *masnawi* form because he provides a dual perspective on things, such as existence-nonexistence, body-soul, and the like, and the couplets echo this. Rumi uses alternative names for the work in the *Masnawi* itself: "The Polish for Souls," "*Husaminama*," "The Discoverer of the Qur'an," and "The Great Book of Jurisprudence."

As we have mentioned before, the book was written as a result of a request by Husameddin Chelebi. The data available today helps us to infer an approximate date when the *Masnawi* was written, that is, the second volume of the work was probably finished in 1264. According to Aflaki, there is a two-year gap between the first two volumes due to the death of Husameddin's wife. Taking this as basis, Sahih Ahmed Dede suggests that Rumi started writing it in May 1261, when he was 55 and Husameddin was 37. Furuzanfar believes that the first volume was written between 1258 and 1261. Golpinarli takes some of the last lines of the first volume into consideration and estimates that it was written before 1258, when the Abbasids lost the caliphate. Accordingly, the gap between the two volumes becomes six years. In contrast to the first two, the other volumes were written without any lapse. Sahih Ahmed Dede is of the opinion that the last volume was finished in 1268. In short, the entire work seems to have been completed in 8 to 10 years.

Rumi himself gives some details about the process of writing the *Masnawi*. It is understood that Rumi himself did not actually put pen to paper, and he did not consult any books. He dictated it almost everywhere—wherever he was, from the *madrasa* to the public bath. Sometimes, he would stop for a few days; other times, he would utter nothing but the lines of the *Masnawi*. Sometimes the writing would last until the morning and Husameddin would not be able to sleep. Then, when Rumi ate something, his inspiration became blurred. After completing every volume, Husameddin read what he had written back to Rumi to have it corrected. Rumi, in return, praised his hardworking disciple as a light from God, and dedicated the *Masnawi* to him. The preface and the titles were written in red ink after each volume was completed. Rumi himself ordered for them to be written. Aflaki notes that Sultan Walad and some others helped Husameddin Chelebi with the writing. Also, according to Salih Ahmed Dede, the story of the three princes in volume six was completed by Sultan Walad. However, the present version of the story is still incomplete.

The *Masnawi* is an original work which is a fruit of Rumi's genius. However, in terms of style and understanding, it can be viewed as a continuation of a line that includes Sanai and Attar. In spite of his extraordinary talent in languages and poetry, Rumi complains about his inability to express his feelings and enthusiasm. In his opinion, poetry is nothing more than a means of expression which one is compelled to resort to, as there is no better option. He notes that meanings are not fully contained by words; but he also adds that making use of tools like poetry and stories is obligatory if one wants to attempt to reveal meanings. (*Masnawi*, vol. VI, 160)

In every preface, the topics of the relevant volume are summarized. For example, the preface of the first volume presents topics such as Islamic rules, Sufism, and the truth. Through practices, such as making ablutions, observing the prayers, fasting, and the like, a certain path is taken—one that takes an initiate toward the truth. Rumi wrote freely, and he did not hesitate to use fables and humorous stories among his narration techniques. He explains the reason why he did so:

> *All my couplets are a climate of wisdom,*
> *All these stories teach a lesson.*

Sipahsalar asserts that even if the *Masnawi* seems to be just poetry, it holds the secrets of Divine Unity, which is a guide for Sufis, a reflection of the Qur'an, a key to understanding the *hadith*s, and the essence of fundamental truths. Rumi himself describes the *Masnawi* as an expounder that clarifies some of the inner meanings of the Qur'an. Research into the *Masnawi* verifies this description; for among the 950 topics, more than 50 are verses and 53 of them are *hadith*. Although there is not much direct reference to the *hadith*s or verses in the text, these two are always the source of inspiration. In conclusion, we can say that the *Masnawi* is the most brilliant representative of Sufi works which aim to serve spiritual progress. Its topics will be discussed further in a separate chapter.

Different Versions and Translations

The oldest copy of the *Masnawi* that has reached us today is the one in the Rumi Museum in Konya. It is Sultan Walad's version and is registered as "Item Number 51." It was written five years after Rumi's death by Muhammad bin Abdullah, of Konya, one of Sultan Walad's dervishes. It includes 25668 couplets and is based on rough drafts by Husameddin Chelebi. A facsimile of this manuscript was published by the Turkish Ministry of Culture in 1993. A comparison with the far more voluminous versions published in Iran and India—some up to 32,000 couplets—gives an idea of the fabricated additions to the original text that have compromised the integrity of Rumi's poetry and cast some doubts on the true perception of this gifted figure as an uncompromising believer who submitted himself entirely to God.

In different parts of the world several translations and commentaries on the *Masnawi* have been produced. Gulshehri, the first translator known in Anatolia, included some stories from the *Masnawi* in his own works, *Falaknama* and *Mantiqut Tayr*. The first complete commentary on the *Masnawi* was written in Persian by Sururi, a 16ᵗʰ-century scholar of the art of eloquence. In turn, commentators like Sudi and Sami wrote their analyses in Turkish. But the most comprehensive and esteemed work belongs to Ismail Ankaravi. In his text, *Majmuatul Lataif*, Ankaravi benefited from *Futuhatul Makkiya*. The first edition was printed in 1806 CE in Cairo, and it was also translated into Arabic. The main drawback of this work is that it includes Volume Seven, which has been proven to be fabricated. There are also various studies on the *Masnawi* in both Turkey and Iran.

Masnawi studies have had quite a long history in the West. The earliest example we know of is the translation of the first 18 verses by Sir William Jones (d. 1794 CE). The first translation into French was made by Jacques van Wallenbourg (d. 1806), but the text was destroyed in the great fire in Pera (1799).

Undoubtedly, Goethe played an importance role in raising interest in the *Masnawi* in Germany. Goethe was interested in Persian poetry and in the works of Hafiz in particular. He also mentioned Rumi in a few lines. According to Schimmel, however, Goethe's knowledge of Rumi was insufficient and lacked understanding. In contrast, Muhammad Iqbal beautifully expressed in his poem, *Payami Mashriq*, that the most profound ideas of these two poets are basically in agreement. (Schimmel, 2002, 28). The first translation in German was made by Hammel. However, despite finding this translation accurate, Schimmel criticizes how the dry expressions fail to reflect the beauty of the original text. On the other hand, F. Rückert saw the light of Rumi upon reading Hammer's translation. Impressed by what he read, he wrote nearly sixty poems under the pen name "Mavlana Jalaluddin," and he dedicated them to Rumi, whom he described as "the mystical sun that rose in the West."

Edward Henry Whinfield successfully translated 3,500 couplets from the *Masnawi* into English, picked from different parts of the work. The complete text and its translation was published for the first time in the West thanks to Reynold Nicholson. Later on, his student, Arthur John Arberry, made contributions to this work. The second complete *Masnawi* translation in English belongs to M. G. Gupta. The following people also have made significant contributions to the interpretation of the *Masnawi*: Helmut Ritter, Hans Meinke, Jan Rypka, Annemarie Schimmel, Kaveh Dalir Azar, and Eva de Vitray-Meyerovitch. Partially or completely, the *Masnawi* has been translated into a number of languages, such as English, French, Italian, Spanish, Japanese, and Bosnian.

Along with these, there are some popular adaptations. The adaptations by Coleman Barks—although he secularizes the Sufi metaphors—are remarkable. Additionally, the translation/adaptation by Kabir and Camille Helminski raised particular interest in the United States.

DIVANI KABIR (THE DIVAN OF SHAMS) AND OTHERS

The immense work that bears witness to the eternal inspiration of Rumi is *Divani Kabir*. It was given this title, which means, "the great collection of poems," owing to its huge volume, which is 8 to 10 times greater than an average *divan* (collection of poems).

Nearly all the poems in the corpus were uttered by Rumi spontaneously during the *sama*. Later, others wrote these poems down
and classified them according to the 21 types of the *aruz* metric
form. Rumi thought that it was Shams who inspired him to speak.
Therefore, he named this work the *Divan of Shams*. Being a faithful friend, Rumi also used the names of Salahaddin Zarqubi and
Husameddin Chelebi in some other *ghazals*.[10] In a few poems, he
used the penname, "Hamush." In both his *Divan* and the *Masnawi*,
Rumi used common Persian. There are a few poems in Arabic and
Greek, as well. He recited his poems spontaneously, in a free-flow
of inspiration. Despite having pushed all the opportunities that
poetry presents to the limits, he complained about the rules that
restricted him, such as rhyme and measure. Even though his *ghazals* sometimes reach up to 80 or 90 lines, they maintain a unity of
meaning rarely found in classical *ghazals*.

Along with being works of great knowledge and wisdom, the
local elements in the poems constitute a rich source, giving an idea
about the age in which they were written. Being a keen observer,
Rumi depicts the traditions, beliefs, and various life scenes from his
age like a master artist, with a few strokes of his brush. The similarity of some of his poems to masters like Mutanabbi, Sanai, Attar,
Rudagi, Nasiri Husrav, and Khayyam are important in terms of
establishing Rumi's familiarity with them. The number of couplets
in the *Divani Kabir* varies in different versions, from 30,000 to
50,000. An academic version was published by Furuzanfar, in
Tehran, 1336. He collected 1,765 quatrains in eight volumes.

Fihi Mafih

Rumi's talks were recorded by Sultan Walad and a number of other disciples. *Fihi Mafih* is a posthumous compilation of these notes.
Six of the seventy-five chapters—seventy-six in some versions—are
in Arabic, while the rest are in Persian. The book consists of sermons, questions and answers. The subjects are parallel to the
Masnawi. It was published in Iran by Furuzanfar.

Majalisi Saba (The Seven Pieces of Advice)

This is a compilation of Rumi's sermons and counsels. In this work he explains certain verses and *hadith*s. There are also poems from famous poets like Sanai and Attar, some stories that are told in the *Masnawi*, and select poems from *Divani Kabir*.

Maktubat (Rumi's Letters)

As the name suggests, this book is compiled from Rumi's letters, which he wrote to different people for various reasons. He wrote some of these to his relatives, children, and dervishes—but the majority of the letters were written to the authorities to convey the demands of the needy. The most trustworthy version of Rumi's letters was published by Tawfik Subhani, in 1992.

In addition to these books, there are two books of prayers that are thought to have been compiled by Rumi: *Awradi Kabir*, and *Awradi Saghiri Hazreti Mevlana* (1885).

PRAISES FOR RUMI AND THE MASNAWI

Rumi:

> *Our Masnawi is a shop of divine oneness,*
> *Whatever you see there, other than One, it's a false-idol.*

Molla Jami

> *Whoever reads the Masnawi in the morning and evening,*
> *That person will be safe from the fire of Hell.*

Muhammad Iqbal

> *Rumi is completely love and heat,*
> *And I am the ash of this fire.*

Halifa Abdul Hakim:

"Although the works of Sufis share the same philosophy, the way Rumi feels and senses is incomparably superior to all others."

E. Browne:

"Undoubtedly, Rumi is the greatest of all Sufi poets, and his *Mathnawi* deserves to be called the best poetry of all times."

Joseph von Hammer:

"The *Masnawi* is a pocketbook for all Sufis, from the river Ganges to the coasts of the Bosphorus."

Reynold Nicholson (his last words upon his death bed):

"Rumi, now I understand you better."

A.J. Arberry:

"I will devote the rest of my life to studying Rumi's works; one can find there spiritual cures and consolations for the diseases of our age."

Irene Melikoff:

"If the nations of the world were to translate Rumi's works into their own languages and read them, there would be no war, grudges, or hatred in the world."

M. Barres:

"I couldn't contain my excitement. I was looking forward to visiting the dervish lodge, the *sama* ground, and the tomb of Rumi—to feel his divine love, to hear the melody of his poems."

Both in the East and West, there are various studies on Rumi. The following can be considered as the most notable ones:

John Renard, *All the King's Falcons: Rumi on Prophets and Revelation*, New York: 1994.

Afzal Iqbal, *The Life and Work of Jalaluddin Rumi*, Pakistan: 1999

Reza Arasteh, *Rumi, the Persian, the Sufi*, London: 1974.

Franklin D. Lewis, *Rumi, Past and Present, East and West: The Life, Teachings, and Poetry of Jalal al-Din Rumi*, Oxford: 2000.

Jalal Humai, *Mawlawinama: The Thoughts and Ideas of Mawlana*, Tehran, 1983.

Khalifa Abdul Hakim, *The Metaphysics of Rumi: A Critical and Historical Sketch*, Lahore, 1965

Annemarie Schimmel, *The Triumphal Sun: A Study of the Works of Jalaladdin Rumi*, London, 1980

———*I Am Wind, You Are Fire: The Life and Work of Rumi*, Boston: 1992.

William C. Chittick, *The Sufi Doctrine of Rumi: An Introduction; The Sufi Path of Love: The Spiritual Teachings of Rumi*, Albany, 1983.

Krish Khosla, *The Sufism of Rumi*, Longmead: 1987.

LISTEN TO RUMI

Listen,
To the Masnawi and to Rumi,
To the ney which tells you about yourself.
Listen to the ney,
To the Masnawi and Rumi—
It is not of the voices you know.
Understand where you come from, and where you are going,
And know the meaning of being human.
Listen to the ney
To the Masnawi and Rumi,
So that those sounds that come from the heart
Will tell you, like the Holy Spirit:[11]
"You are also a Mary, please listen,
And give birth to the Jesus blown into your soul."

CHAPTER 3

UNDERSTANDING RUMI
IN PARABLES

No matter the era in which we live there are some essential questions that never lose their importance: Who am I? Where do I come from, and where am I going? Who has sent me to this world, and what does He require of me? The following quotation from *Fihi Mafih* seems to reply to the questions above:

We need to know that there is only one thing in the world that should not be forgotten. Do not worry if you forget everything as long as you do not forget God. However, if you do everything, but you forget Him, you will be considered as having done nothing. This can be explained with the following comparison: If a ruler sends you to a country with a certain duty to fulfill, and you ignore your essential duty but do many other things instead, you will have done everything in vain. Man has come to this world for a certain deed. If you say: "I am not fulfilling my duty, but I do many other things," woe to you! You have not been created for any other deed!

In Rumi's works we are invited on a spiritual journey to find the answers to these questions. A part of the journey is related to our inner world, while the other part is related to the outer world. Then let us answer the call for answers that transcends the ages, and follow the track. In the person of an imaginary initiate, we will ask these same questions of a Sufi master, and he will try to help us through the wisdom of Rumi. Let us drop by the gardens of the *Masnawi* for a time, and then satisfy our thirst from the fountains of *Fihi Mafih*. And from time-to-time, let us lend an ear to the *Divani Kabir,* or the *Majalisi Saba*.

I. Who Am I?

Let us reconsider the matter posed in the quotation above of a man who is sent to perform a certain task in a certain country. Obviously, the ruler denotes God Almighty, we are the servants, and this world is the country we have been sent to. But what about our principal duty? There is no evident answer given in the analogy. Yet the answer to this is hidden in the works of Rumi and in the *Masnawi*, in particular. Thus, we can try to find that hidden answer and clarify it. For a start, it can be summarized thus: we came into this world as human beings, and we are supposed to return to the eternal abode where we came from as decent people. Undoubtedly, this is the essential duty which the Ruler expects us to fulfill. Recall that the answer which Rumi's father, Baha Walad, gave in Baghdad to those who asked where they had come from and where they were going was simply this: "We have come from God, and we are returning to Him again." For this is the only true journey, and all other journeys ultimately lead to this prime one. At this point, Rumi hands us a road map to guide us through this journey. On that map, he introduces us to the path of true humanity with the perils marked out along the way, and he gives us tips to save us from loss and danger. But above all, he holds out a comprehensive mirror to let us examine ourselves first. Then let the initiate begin a dialogue with such a teacher:

– Who am I?

– O human being; you are both a beast and an angel! The animal-like body and the angel-like soul came together and united in you. Therefore, you belong to both the heavens and the earth. (*Masnawi*, 2:3814)

God created angels and granted them reason. He created animals, and granted them carnal desires. Then He created man, and granted him both reason and carnal desires. If your reason overcomes your carnal desires, you are better than the angels. But if your carnal desires overcome your reason, then you are lowlier than the animals." (*Masnawi*, 4:59)

– Then my nature consists of body and soul. So, what are their due values with respect to each other? What is it that makes me worth being called human?

– The body is to the soul what a purse is to the gold it holds.

The value of a purse is the gold it contains,
Without the gold, the purse is abtar.[12]

Likewise, the value of the body comes from the soul it possesses and the value of the soul comes from the light of God shining on it. (*Masnawi*, 3:2546)

Thanks to your thoughts, "human" they call you
Flesh and bones hold no value.

It is the spirit that matters, not the body. Look—when the soul leaves the body, they do not even let it stay at home, they just bury it quickly. (Furuzanfar, 126)

Another comparison can be made thus: your situation is like that of a pearl, or a jug of water. Not every oyster contains a pearl. O my dear, do not be deceived by the shiny mother-of-pearl, but try to see the pearl itself. How long will you waste time with the decorations on the jug? Forget about the decorations, and seek water! (*Masnawi*, 2:38)

– Man consists of clay, namely soil and water—is that true?

– That's right. Man consists of soil and water—but a matured person is like clear water filtered of its soil. Clear water reveals pebbles and stones, and whatever else there is at the bottom; it reveals neither more nor less. But if it is mixed with soil, then it becomes muddy. The prophets and saints are like clear, immense bodies of water. When clouded water sees them, it says, "Then my nature is not muddy. My essential nature must be clear, like theirs," and they long to join them. As these small and muddy bodies join the sea, they become pure and clear. However, the water that keeps separate and does not join the sea remains muddy. Then its essence is water. Seemingly, there is something that separates the smaller body of water from the greater one, and this is soil." (Furuzanfar, 48)

– Soil and water…, the shell and the pearl… In short, I hold both the worthy and worthless within me!

– Correct. With this dual nature of yours, you are both the smallest, and the greatest world.

With respect to appearance, you are the smallest world,
With respect to meaning, you are the greatest world. (Masnawi, 4:531)

– People are similar in appearance. But if their inner values make them so different, then does a human appearance suffice to make us human?

– Of course not. If it did, it would mean:

If being human in appearance were sufficient,
Muhammad and Abu Jahl [13] would be no different (Masnawi, 1:1060)
Though their arms, head, and body look the same,
Moses is high in heaven, but the Pharaoh is the lowliest one. (Masnawi, 6:3032)

– If outward appearance is misleading, how can we understand a person's true worth?

– In order to find out what something is, you need to look at its essence. If you make candy in the shape of bread, it isn't bread, but still candy. To know whether it is bread or candy, you need to taste it; the eye does not recognize taste. Then do not consider any person who looks like candy by looking only at the person's shape. (*Masnawi*, 1:2980) In short:

Similarity of words always misleads,
As a pagan and a believer have similar bodies.
Their bodies are like jugs with closed lids.
Though both jugs have some ornamentation,
One of them holds the water of life,
While the other holds deadly poison. (Masnawi, vol.6, 666)

In other words, man can be compared to a tree, and a tree that yields fruit is better than a hundred trees that do not yield any fruit. (Furuzanfar, 71)

We have been talking about the dual nature of man. But if having both a body and a soul is a requirement of my being human, then why should I deny a part of my nature, ignoring its existence?

– It is not a matter of denying or ignoring its existence—it is just a question of who is in control. You have both Jesus and the donkey he rides within you. The donkey is your material being, your untrained nature. Your reason and spirit are like Jesus who rides the donkey. You are supposed to value Jesus, not the donkey. Do not put your ego—which is like a donkey—above your reason—which is like Prophet Jesus. Let your body serve your soul, and run after high ideals. (*Masnawi,* 2:1871)

Look—a horse has eyes, so does a king. A good horse does not see through its own eyes, but it sees though the king's eyes. So, too, your eyes must be like an obedient horse; they should abide by the rule of mind and insight. (*Masnawi,* 2:247)

– All right, but the horse's eye and the king's eye—or carnal self and logic—do they always have to contradict each other? Can't they ever be at peace?

– This is a demand in vain. Since your body is your horse, this world is its barn. The fodder of the horse cannot be the food of the rider. The food, nourishment, and sleep of the rider are different. However, you continue to live in the barn for your carnal self has overcome you. (Furuzanfar, 24) The situation of the body and soul which constantly try to trip up each other is like Majnun and his camel.

Majnun and his camel

Majnun was riding his camel with the hope of reaching Layla. He longed for Layla, but the camel longed for the young she had left behind. Whenever Majnun fell asleep, the camel would feel the bridle loosen. Then she would immediately return and run back for her young. After traveling like this for some time, Majnun saw that they were still traveling in the same area. He sighed deeply and said, "O camel, we both are in love, but our beloved ones are different. The way to reunion just takes two days, but because of you, I've wasted my sixty-year lifetime trapped on the way." (*Masnawi,* 4:60)

– This means that God gives us some things which we are supposed to be wary of. Then why have we been given a carnal self and lust? What can be the wisdom behind this?

– They have been given to you as a test, for this world is a testing ground for you. If there were no test, there would be no way to separate who's raw and who's mature.

Can there be a struggle without an enemy? Without the carnal desires blocking our way obedience to God is not appreciated. Then do not try to castrate yourself like a monk; instead, you should try to keep chaste despite your lust. (*Masnawi*, 5:580, 82)

God created angels with pure common sense, and He created beasts with pure carnal desires. One of these was saved by its knowledge, and the other was saved by its ignorance. Man is simply in between. (Furuzanfar, 121) God has assembled both humanity and beastliness within our nature so that one thing will be known through its opposite—so that is the difference between Adam and Satan, Moses and the Pharaoh, Abraham and Nimrod, and the Prophet Muhammad and Abu Jahl. (Furuzanfar, 117)

All these reveal that beauty and ugliness can be evaluated from two perspectives: physical beauty versus spiritual beauty. We do not have the option to choose our body. However, we can shape our own inner world, and we have been enabled toward a good character through the use of our will. This seems to be what really matters.

– Exactly. Rumi says that people care for the ornaments on a wine glass, but I am devoted to the wine[14] it holds. Who would care for a golden goblet if it held vinegar! A squash containing wine is better to me than hundreds of golden goblets full of vinegar. Thus, the physical appearance of people is like the decorations, the depictions engraved on a goblet. When the goblet breaks, no ornament is left; you should prefer what it contains. (Furuzanfar, 107) The same goes for divine judgment. If you want to know how God evaluates us, listen to the following parable:

The physically ugly and the spiritually ugly

A certain king had two slaves. One of them was not good looking, but he had a good character; and the other had a bad character, but was very handsome. The king gave a task to the handsome one and sent him away. He told the other, "I know you to be a clever and skillful slave, but your friend is gossiping about you. He says that you are a thief and that you are very mean. What do you have to say about this?" He tried to provoke the good slave against his friend and make him gossip. But the slave gave an exemplary reply, "Your majesty! All the words of my friend are true. I can even say that I am worse than he describes me. It seems that he has hidden most of my faults out of kindness." On hearing this, the king ordered him, "All right, now just as he told me about your faults, you tell me about his." The slave replied, "His faults are love, faithfulness, generosity, self-sacrifice, humility...," and he listed all the virtues he knew. After this, the king sent him away with a duty and summoned the handsome slave. He repeated what he said to the first one: "The other slave told me so many bad things about you. However, I don't see any such qualities in you. On the contrary, I find you clever and skillful." On hearing this, the handsome slave flew into a rage. He praised himself and also sputtered every word to insult his friend. In return for this, the king expelled him, saying, "You mean-spirited one! His face is unattractive, but his inside is so pure. You, however, have a good-looking face, but your heart is corrupt and rotten! Get away from me right now!" (*Masnawi*, 2:32)

– The story is very meaningful. I take it that it is not that easy to be a human being in the true sense of the word.

– Surely not. The following parable also tells us about this.

Looking for a true human being

There was a priest who walked throughout the streets and markets with a lamp in his hand. A fool approached him and asked, "Why are you walking around with a lamp in the middle of the day?" The priest answered, "I am looking for a human being." The fool continued, "That's strange. Don't you see that there are people every-where?" So the priest exclaimed, "No, no. This isn't what I mean. I am looking for a true human being. I wish I could find him, and become the soil under his feet." (*Masnawi*, 5:118)

II. Degrees of Humanity

– Given that we fulfill the requirement of being human with our spirit and intellect, then we can say that there are as many degrees of humanity as there are people.

– Certainly. According to Rumi, there is a secret stairway in this world which ascends up to the heavens. Each person occupies a different step, according to his or her spiritual level. (*Masnawi*, 5:2565)

We cannot learn about everyone individually. So if we were to separate the inhabitants of the stairs into a few groups, what would be the major types of people?

– We can roughly group them as the raw ones and the mature ones—those who know and those who don't—as patients and doc-tors, or as travelers and guides. Also, we shouldn't forget the pseu-do-mature, the patients who look like doctors, and the impostors.

According to Rumi, being a child or adult is not dependent on age; it is a matter of maturity. Those who run after childish fancies are like children, no matter how old they are.

> *Only those intoxicated with divine love are worth being called adults.*
> *Those who run after their fancies cannot be considered to be grown-ups.*
> (Masnawi, 1:3536)

On the other hand, neither the disease nor the treatment is confined only to the body. Most people are ill in terms of their views, thoughts, and beliefs. The true doctors are those who cure the spirit. They tell their patients: "We are doctors who receive our knowledge not from medical books, but from God. Physicians only cure physical diseases. We, on the other hand, cure diseased spirits. We don't ask for any wages for treatment, unlike physicians. Our wages are due only from God. Then come,

O desperate patients! We have the cure for all of your diseases."
(*Masnawi,* 4:70)

– Children, adults, patients and doctors...yet, there is another
grouping with respect to knowledge and the use of the intellect,
isn't there?

– Yes, there is. Through the long and dark journey in this
world, the light of the mind should illuminate our way—but minds
are infinitely different:

> *Minds are ranked in accordance with their capacities—*
> *Their levels differ from the ground, up to the heavens.* (Masnawi, 5:461)

Despite the infinity of differences of their minds, people fall
into three main groups with respect to the ability of their intellect:
the intelligent, the semi-intelligent, and the non-intelligent. The
intelligent are enlightened with their own inner light. With this
light, they both enlighten their own way and guide a community.
This is the intellect of a mature believer, an intellect that leaves no
place for any doubts. The semi-intelligent ones, without their own
light to show the way, can still use their common-sense and see
through the eyes of the guide. Those in the third group are utterly
blind; they neither have their own intellect, nor do they follow an
intelligent guide. Therefore, they are in the pitch dark. They try to
pass through vast plains limping, and they roam in vain. (*Masnawi,*
4:84) Look, thousands of soldiers covering large plains are under
the command of a single commander. But an ordinary commander
can be obsessed by a worthless thought. If so many people obey
one who has such worthless ideas, then what kind of obedience
should be shown to a worthy ideal? Imagine! (Furuzanfar, 87)

– It is understood that the infinite diversity between people in
terms of their knowledge and ethical levels renders some people to
be teachers while others are students—but how far does this
teacher-student relationship go?

– Naturally, there will be other teachers, other guides, above
every teacher. The greatest teachers of humanity are the prophets;
their teacher is God Almighty Himself. For this reason, their

knowledge is the absolute truth, and salvation is in the direction to
which they point. Nevertheless, God's Messenger said: "I and my
Companions are like the Noah's Ark; we are the shelter for salvation." (*Masnawi*, 4:22) Being a shelter can be explained thus: If a
horse falls into a salt cellar it will turn to salt after a certain time.
Even if it still looks like a horse, it is not a horse anymore, in reality. Even if you give it a different name, salt is salt. A person who
annuls his own being in God still exists physically; but in reality, the
One who acts is God. (Furuzanfar, 88)

– In this case, there must be duties that fall on both sides. The
guide should be a good guide, and the traveler should surrender to
the guide—is that it?

– This is the ideal, but it isn't always what happens in practice.
Rumi explains this through the following example: "If they tie two
birds together, they cannot fly away, in spite of flapping the four
wings they have. But if one of the birds is dead, the living one can
carry the other. So it means that to take wing with the guide one
should kill his ego. How can a guide fly with a person who trusts
only his own mind? (Furuzanfar, 36)

Great guides are full of compassion and affection for people,
like shepherds protecting the herd which is under their responsibility. Those who cannot surrender to this affection endanger themselves and also make the guide tired from running after them. Here
is a story that touches on this very point:

Moses and the runaway sheep

Once, a sheep ran away from Moses' herd. Moses was anxious to
save it from wolves, so he ran after it until the evening. In the end,
he caught the exhausted sheep and began stroking it tenderly. He
said: "Look what has become of my clothes and shoes while running after you! Don't you have any conscience? Why did you make
me run like this? Perhaps you don't care for me—but don't you care
enough about yourself avoid such danger?" Upon this, God
Almighty said to the angels: "Moses has proven worthy of being a

Prophet." Also, Prophet Muhammad said: "There is no Prophet who was not a shepherd in his youth or childhood," for all leaders are the equivalent of shepherds with respect to caring for the people under their responsibility. (*Masnawi*, 6:122) Sometimes guides persuade people with sweet words, to get them into a straight line, but this does not fool them. A mother persuades her son to do something for his own good. But others try to persuade us into something in order to take advantage of what we have. What a mother, or a prophet, does might seem to be a trick, but it is in reality a blessing. (Furuzanfar, 38)

– Previously, you compared guides to torches that illuminate the way for others. The duty that befalls a traveler must be to hold the guide high, like a torch to show the way.

– This is true, but it should be kept in mind that such high esteem is for the benefit of the traveler, not for the torch. On seeing an ignorant man who came and sat above a scholar, Rumi said: "If the candle wishes to be above, this is not for himself but for the sake of enlightening people better. Otherwise, down or up, he is a candle anyway." (Furuzanfar, 37) The sun is the source of light in any case, but without it, people would be in darkness. (Furuzanfar, 154) If you put gold down on the ground, and put silver on the roof, which one will be superior? Gold, of course! Likewise, even if flour is under the sieve and the chaff remains upon the sieve, the flour still has greater value. The reason why the Prophet conquered so many lands was in order to present the true life and Paradise to others—not to gain power for himself. This is true with regards to all the prophets; "Their hands existed to give, not to take." Actually, those whom God supports do not need the support of people. Look how God makes people glorify His saints. Everybody builds tombs for themselves in order to be remembered or to show their liberality. God, however, displays the worth of His saints through the tombs built by other people in their honor. (Furuzanfar, 157)

– At the beginning, you talked about impostors. Let's conclude with them.

– Right. For those without insight who make baseless claims, Rumi says: "Some say that they have seen, or that they know. Who will believe you if you say you have seen the eye of the needle and threaded it while you even cannot see a camel on the roof! Like a blind man looking out to observe the street, those who are blind with respect to their insight look out from the window of their body, but they just don't see. If the inwardly blind claim to have seen, their claim has no value versus that of the intelligent. (Furuzanfar, 133)

III. The City Called the World

– To some extent we have become familiar with the two basic types of individuals who on the stairs: the raw and the mature. Now I would like to learn about the attitude of these in this world.

– The heedless think that they are merely travelers in this world, and they think themselves to be permanent. Like children, they are so absorbed in the games they play that they neither think of their true country, nor do think about the Ruler who sent them here. Actually, whoever is separated from their original realm becomes homesick and longs for return. However, this longing is only for those who remember their origins. And remembering one's origins depends on the maturity of the soul.

Most people not only forget their original homeland, but they also become enemies of those who remind them of this truth. This world is like a barn which holds hay to eat, and the noble souls who long for the realms beyond can be compared to gazelles put in a barn full of donkeys, as the following story explains.

The gazelle in the donkeys' barn

A hunter caught a fragile gazelle and put him in the barn. The barn was full of oxen and donkeys. The poor gazelle felt dizzy, and he nearly fainted. He ran frantically back and forth, looking for a way out, but the doors were closed tight. In the evening, the owner of the barn brought the animals hay. It was so delicious for the oxen and donkeys, but not for the poor gazelle! Helplessly, he starved in the barn for days, suffered, and kept struggling like a fish out of water. The animals in the barn thought that he refused to eat merely out of arrogance and they sarcastically said, "It is a pity for a king like you to fall into a barn like this!" The poor gazelle spoke to the mocking donkey tied beside him: "Do not think that I don't eat dry hay out of arrogance. It is a normal food for you, but not for me. I grew up in the meadows eating fresh grass and drinking pure water. I even used to be reluctant with the fresh tulips, hyacinths, and sweet basil in my homeland. Though I am now far from my homeland, that doesn't change the fact that I'm still a gazelle! I'm poor, but I'm not poor in spirit; my clothes are shabby but my soul is not." The donkey didn't believe these words and said: "Homesickness sometimes make people speak such nonsense; you need to prove this to make us believe you." Then the gazelle said: "The musk in my belly is evidence for this. That musk did not form just by eating hay—understand that!" (*Masnawi*, 5:34)

– In any case, I don't think that the donkeys cared about what the gazelle said; people do not care about what those who warn them about the Hereafter say.

– They don't, for each person can see, hear, and interpret according to the capacity of their cognition. If the person you're addressing has the cognition of a donkey, how can your words have an influence on him? A man going on pilgrimage was passing by a desert. He was very thirsty when he saw a small tent. He asked for water, but the woman inside offered him water which was hotter than fire and saltier than the sea. When he drank it, he felt it burn from his lips down to his stomach. He pitied the woman and said: "You have been kind to me, and I want to do you a favor in return. There are civilized cities like Basra and Baghdad, not so far away from here. There you can find various sorts of food and water, like sherbet. Even a disabled man can go there, struggling along, with difficulty. Why do you remain stuck here, in this wasteland?" Thus, he counseled her. Soon, the woman's husband, who had hunted a few deserts rats, came along. They offered the meat from the rats they cooked to their guest, and the man ate a little, albeit unwillingly. At night, as he slept outside the tent, the woman conveyed to her husband what the guest had told her and asked him what he thought. The man said: "O woman, don't listen to such words, for there are so many jealous people in the world. They cannot stand seeing others enjoy their blessings, and they try to deprive them of what they have." This is how heedless people take your affection for jealousy, and they lose the true blessings they could have reached with a little effort. (Kabaklı, 334)

– In these parables the worldly blessings are represented with things like hay or rats. Are they really so paltry? If so, don't the efforts of those who strive to possess them deserve pity?

– According to Rumi, you should pity them and say: "O lover of this world! Those who seek will find what they seek, of course. However, I wish what you were seeking was worth your efforts! Your situation is like that of a boar-hunter. The poor hunter exhausts himself, his horse, and his dog chasing the boar. They all become ill and he uses up all his arrows. When he catches the animal, in the end, he learns that neither its meat, nor its skin is of any use at all. Then he throws the carcass aside, regretting his efforts. (*Majalisi Saba*, 64) As another example, you can compare this worldly man to a fox hunting on a drum. The fox sees a drum hanging on a tree. He considers the sound it makes as it hits the branches around, and he tries to figure out how much meat is inside. Thinking about this, he strives to get hold of it all day long. Finally, when he manages to grab it, a thorn pierces the drum and the fox sees that there is nothing inside it except for stench. Then the fox cries over his vain efforts, like the lovers of this world will do on the night of their death. (*Majalisi Saba*, 100)

– A thing's worth is only known by comparing it to something else. So when we say that the world has worth or does not have worth, what is the comparison?

– The worth of this world is with respect to the blessings of the Hereafter. Some lose the things of greater worth while pursuing things in this world. Their situation can be compared to the poor man in the following parable:

Which is worth more, clay or candy?

A glutton became addicted to eating clay. One day he stopped at a shop to buy candy. The deceitful shopkeeper, who knew his weakness, said: "My candies are of good quality, but mind you, I use two lumps of clay as the weights on my scales." So after tempting him with the idea of eating clay, he went inside to prepare the candy. The customer took the opportunity and started gobbling up the clay on the scales. He was also watching out for the shopkeeper. However, the shopkeeper took his time on purpose and said to himself: "You fool! You are afraid of my seeing you, but I am afraid of your eating little. I pretend to be busy, not out of stupidity, but out of cunning. Clay does not compare to candy in worth! I want you to eat more, so that the scales will weigh less, and I will keep the candy for myself." (*Masnawi*, 4:p.26)

As can be seen, the blessings of this world are like clay, and those of the Hereafter are like candy. The man who changes candy in return for clay is a fool to think he is being clever while he loses. It is greatly surprising that human beings are so fond of the deceptive beauties of this world so much, while they are so indifferent to the real beauties. Here is a couplet that speaks of this paradox:

O you who can't show enough patience to refrain from worldly pleasures,
How can you bear being deprived of the Hereafter and the Friend (God)?
(2:3104)

Given that the riches of this world do not have great worth, then those who are rich here are not truly rich.

– Naturally. The one who is satisfied with little is called an ascetic. Listen to this parable and understand what true asceticism is.

Who's an ascetic?

A king addressed a poor dervish thus: "O ascetic!" The dervish replied, "You are the ascetic one, not me." The king asked "Me? How can I be called an ascetic while the whole world is mine?" The dervish said: "No—your share of this world in only some food and

clothes. However, I enjoy both worlds. Thus, you are more deserv-
ing of being called an ascetic with respect to the blessings of the
Hereafter." (Furuzanfar, 28)

– Interesting! Clay seems more valuable than candy, and this
world seems more valuable than the Hereafter to most people—but
how is this possible?

– Because this world is a thief, a deceitful one that utters sweet
words. So many souls have fallen for those sweet words and that
smiling face. Here is another parable.

The thief who steals our lifetime in this world

One day, a storyteller was talking about the tricks of tailors. He told
people how deceitful tailors were and he praised their cunning. He
narrated how tailors are so skilled at stealing from the cloth brought
to them by their customers. A man from Hita could no longer stand
these stories. He grew angry and asked: "Tell me, who is the most
skilled tailor in the city?" The storyteller answered, "There is a tailor called Cigeroglu—he is a matchless trickster and thief." The
assertive man said, "I bet neither he nor any other one can steal
from me—not a piece of thread, let alone cloth." The storyteller
warned him: "Don't be so confident! I know several others who
were far cleverer than you, and they all lost what they had. Instead
of suffering such losses yourself, you had better keep away from
him." As this conversation went on, the man became even more
provoked and said to those who were listening: "Here is my horse,
which I am ready to bet. If the tailor can steal any cloth from me, I
will give you the horse; but if I win the bet, then I will take a horse
from you." The others accepted the bet, and they dispersed. All
night long, the man tossed and turned thinking about the tailor. He
was making plans on how to act, and he tried to develop a plan.
Finally, in the morning, he took a sheet of silken cloth with him and
set off for the tailor's. The tailor met him with respect, and started
his sweet words, like a nightingale singing. The man, however, was
on his guard. Carelessly, he threw the cloth on the counter and

ordered: "Make a warrior's suit for me! The upper part must be close fitting and the lower part loose!" The tailor took measures and calculated how much cloth it would take. While working, he kept telling his customers amusing stories. The tailor spoke on and on, until the customer was not the same angry man who had first stormed in. He began to enjoy the tailor's stories, and he laughed at the funny things being told. When he laughed, his already small eyes became even narrower. And each time his eyes were closed, the tailor took an opportunity to snatch a piece of cloth and hide it. When the first story was over, the poor customer remembered neither why he had come, nor the horse he had readily bet. "Please tell me one more story," he implored. This time, when the tailor told an even funnier story; the man burst into laughter. So the tailor snatched one more piece of cloth, of course. When that story was also finished, the customer again asked for more: "I have never before met a man who could tell such amusing stories. I have had a wonderful time. Please, tell me one more story," he begged. The third story was even funnier than the first two. This time, the customer lay down on the floor, seized by laughter. So the tailor cut and snatched an even greater piece from the cloth, saying to himself, "What a pity! This poor man cannot see what is to his own benefit or loss. He is so amused by entertaining stories, just like a child. What can be more ridiculous to you than your own condition! This life cuts away the cloth of children like you who never grow up, even when they reach one hundred!" The third story finished as well. When the man asked for a fourth one, the tailor pitied him and said: "You poor man! I have many stories, but if I keep telling you more, the remaining cloth will not even make a vest, let alone a suit. If you had known the truth, you would have cried bitterly instead of laughing." (*Masnawi*, 6:64) So this world is just like that deceitful tailor, and carnal pleasures are like the amusing stories. As for your lifetime, it is the silken cloth. The real skill is to make a good suit for the Hereafter out of that cloth. If you cannot, your situation will be like that of the snow trader of Nishabur. This poor man put the snow out in the open. No one bought the snow and it melted away. He was crying in the end, saying: "We have no goods left, and nobody has bought any." (*Majalisi Saba*, 15)

– Then the genuine waste is wasting this life.

– Exactly. As Rumi puts it, "My dear, you consider wastefulness as being extravagant with some money, with a few donkey loads of wheat, or a generous inheritance. True wastefulness, however, is wasting your life, for an hour from your lifetime cannot be brought back even for a hundred dinars." (*Majalisi Saba*, 42)

– One who has read all these might infer that we should turn our backs on our worldly life. Is that what we're supposed to do?

– Of course not!

– So what is meant by "worldliness" which we should keep away from?

> Worldliness means being oblivious to the Almighty—
> It does not mean having clothes, money, or family. (Masnawi, I, 1024)

So we are not supposed to distance ourselves from our occupations or our families. The essential point is to not to allow them to encourage or let you forget God, and not to let them lead you into heedlessness. Your lawful gains spent for charity, as well, will be provisions for you in the Hereafter. Nevertheless, God's Messenger said: "Lawful property is a blessing for a righteous person." The wealthy one has should be like the water on which a ship floats. The ship can go towards its destination with the help of the water; but if the water gets inside, the ship will sink. Then wealth is no longer a blessing and it will instead become a burden. Anyway, one should refrain from being greedy about worldly possessions. "Don't you see that most kings do not live as long as their servants do? Even a rose loses its petals earlier than other flowers, for it drinks more of the transient water." (*Majalisi Saba*, 190)

IV. Reason, Knowledge, and Types of Knowledge

– We have learned how the people on the stairs of humanity are different in terms of their attitudes towards this world. Now let us return to the beginning and become acquainted with the light that illuminates the way for the travelers in the desert. You called it the light of mind, didn't you?

– Right, the mind is like a torch, and knowledge is its light. This light illuminates the way in the darkness of the night. There is an even stronger light, which we call love. But let us stay within the line of reason and knowledge. The essential purpose of man is to mature, and this cannot be achieved without knowledge. Not all kinds of knowledge are the same, though. Therefore, one needs to know which kind of knowledge is worthy.

– Then my first question is about the quality of worthy knowledge.

First, knowledge must be useful and enlightening. Here is a parable clarifying this point:

The linguist and the sailor

An arrogant linguist boarded a ship. He asked the sailor, "O sailor, do you know any grammar?" When the other replied in the negative, he said with contempt, "What a pity—you have spent half of your life in vain." This made the sailor sad, but he kept quiet. After a while, a terrible storm broke out and the ship began to sink. The sailor asked the now-frantic linguist, "O grammarian, do you know how to swim?" This time, the linguist replied in the negative. Then the sailor said "What a pity—for it means that you will lose your entire life!" So the moral of the story is that every type of knowledge cannot be used everywhere. If you are on the sea, knowing grammar will be of no use to you. In addition, relying on your own knowledge instead of annihilating your ego and surrendering to God means that you assume individual existence. As water first drowns a man, and then sweeps over its head, so you should be like a dead man, letting the water carry you. Otherwise, if you trust your own knowledge and abilities, it will be very hard for you to be saved from this sea. (*Masnawi*, 1:112)

– So what is the relationship between knowledge and good character?

– One needs to know that knowledge doesn't always bring about the same outcome. It is good in the hands of the good, and it is bad in the hands of the evil.

> *Teaching science to one who is not worthy of it*
> *Can be compared to giving a sword to a bandit.* (Masnawi, 4:1456)

Knowledge brings responsibility to the knower. Therefore, some people's not knowing is better for themselves and for others. Now let us see how knowledge can be disastrous when possessed by one who isn't worthy of knowing:

The fool who wanted to learn the language of the animals

A foolish man begged Prophet Moses, "Please teach me the language of the animals." Moses replied, "O, poor man, why do you wish for such a thing? You had better abandon this idea; you will not be able to handle it. Knowledge brings disaster if you are not capable of using it. The man insisted and said, "Even if you don't teach me all the languages of the animals, please just teach me two of them." Upon this demand, Moses taught him the languages of chickens and dogs. The foolish man happily went home. After dinner, the servant took the tablecloth and shook out the remnants in the garden. The rooster came and started pecking at the crumbs. The dog protested, "This isn't fair! I can't eat grains like you do, and now you are eating the bread I should eat." The rooster answered, "Don't worry— tomorrow you will find better food. Tomorrow, our owner's horse is going to die and you will eat of the carcass." Their owner, who heard this, went to the market right away and sold the horse, so the horse would die in someone else's possession. The fool thought he had made profit, but he was unaware that he was inviting greater danger. The next day, he eavesdropped on the two animals talking under his window again. The rooster was saying, "Don't worry, this time our owner's female slave is going to die. There will be a dinner after the funeral. You will feast on the remaining bones." The man was very pleased with his slave, but on hearing this he immediately sold her as well, thinking he was being saved from great damage. He told him-

self how fortunate he was to have learned the language of the animals. On the third day, the starving dog had become quite thin. The
dog became cross with the rooster, "You are deceiving me! None of
your predictions came true!" The rooster replied, "Actually, I'm very
surprised too, since lying is out of the question for us. We are a
species held in esteem by God and His Messenger, since we wake
people up for prayer. For a few days, strange things have been happening. I can't understand it either. But don't worry, anyway, because
tomorrow your owner is going to die, and the relatives who get the
inheritance will give a feast, for sure. You will certainly have a share
from this as well. Upon hearing this, the man was shocked. He had
sold the horse and the maid, but he could in no way get rid of death
by selling himself! Little misfortunes were compensation in return
for his own life and a barricade between death and himself. Evading
them, one by one, he was now facing the Angel of Death. So the
foolish man hurried to Moses, anxious for his life: "Help me, O
Moses, help me! Take away this knowledge from me, and save me
from this calamity!" Moses said "Alas, as an arrow shot from a bow
does not return, neither does the divine decree. Now what needs to
be done is to pray to God to save your faith." Here, then, is the case
of knowledge possessed by one who is not eligible. Even if such a
man meets Prophet Moses, he does not see this as an opportunity to
revive his spirituality. Instead, he serves his carnal self and uses the
knowledge granted to him as an axe with which to dig his own
grave. (*Masnawi*, 4:125)

– In addition to the perils of abusing knowledge, we also
understand from the story that what matters, in reality, is being able
to separate what one needs and what one doesn't. Am I correct?

– Certainly. The knowledge which one doesn't need and does-
n't know how to use is a burden for a person. Those who possess
useless knowledge are like "donkeys loaded with books." No matter how much you know, you will still *not* be considered knowl-
edgeable in that you cannot benefit from it.

– So I take that seeing, or knowing, something is not always
the same.

– True. Every bad trait of a person is an obstacle for the eye and the ear. Therefore, they are not supposed to know, hear, or understand everything. Such people can be compared to the three people in the following story:

A blind man with keen sight, a deaf man with keen hearing, and a naked man with a long dress

There were three people among the people of Saba. One of them could see very far away, but he was blind. He could see an ant, but he couldn't see Prophet Solomon. The second one heard very well, but he was deaf. He was a treasure, without any gold. And the other one was naked but his dress was long. Sounds strange, right? But what is the point being made here? Let us listen to Rumi's explanation in the *Masnawi*:

"One who owns long-term ambitions is deaf. He hears about the death of others, but he is deaf with respect to his own death. And criticism is blind. It lists the faults of others in detail. With respect to seeing one's own faults, it is blind. As for the naked one, he is afraid that he will lose his dress! How surprising—is it possible for a person who is already naked to lose his dress? People in this world do not own anything, but they are afraid of being robbed. Why should someone who is bankrupt and broke be afraid of thieves? Humans come into this world naked, and they will also leave it naked. So then why should people be anxious, worrying about thieves? It is like a man who has some property in his dream and trembles with fear of thieves. When someone wakes him up, he laughs at his own situation." (*Masnawi*, 3:100) The conclusion to be drawn from all of these narrations is that knowing yourself should be the priority. Everything begins with knowing ourselves, yet it is usually ourselves that we know the least. The *Masnawi* draws attention to this conflict: "A scholar might know thousands of disciplines, but he does not know his own self. Although you have learned what you should and what you shouldn't do, I wonder which one your self pursues! You know the worth of every object, but you are a fool for not knowing your own worth. You even know which stars are regarded as fortunate and which ones are not, but you are unaware of whether *you* are fortunate or not." (3:101)

– Leaving what you don't need to know, and ignoring what you do—that's quite interesting! Is there one more example of useless knowledge?

– There are actually many. But as a drop can give an idea of the sea, a small example will suffice:

The knowledge of the foolish prince

A king sent his foolish son to join a group of academics. They taught many things to the prince, and he became a scholar. One day, the king took an object in his palm and wanted to test his son: "Tell me what is in my hand," he commanded. The boy said, "There is something round, hollow, and yellow." The king was pleased: "Right—you know its features. Then do you know what it is?" The prince replied, "A sieve!" The king was surprised, as he exclaimed, "You know so many details, yet you do not know that a sieve is too big to hold in my palm!"

According to Rumi, this is what has become of scholars. They know about things that don't concern them in great detail, but they are not aware of the closest thing; that is, they do not know themselves! Further, being yellow, round, and hollow are relative attributes, for when thrown into a fire, none of these characteristics remain—only the essence remains. (Furuzanfar, 26)

In sum,

The knowledge of people who are sound at heart carries the owner,
While the knowledge of hedonists is a burden which the owner carries.
(1:3552)

Along with the matter of unnecessary knowledge, are there not also those who don't know but pretend to know, just repeating the words of others from time to time?

– That is right, but such assumed knowledge and borrowed words are of no use for the owner. The difference between the true possessor of knowledge and an imitator can be compared to that of a dog and her puppies:

The puppies that barked in the womb

One day, a dervish in retreat had a dream in which unborn puppies were barking in their mother's womb. Astonished at their barking, he said to himself, "They can neither chase away a wolf, nor a thief! They can neither join a hunt, nor guard a house! Then, what is the point of their barking?" A voice said: "This resembles the words of those who speak without knowledge." (*Masnawi*, 5:59)

So we need to think with our own minds, and fly with our own wings.

Take a look, free of imitation—
Give up others' minds, and think with your own. (Masnawi, 6:3371)

Knowledge which belongs to someone else is like water coming to a castle from outside. It is good in peacetime, but in wartime, it can be cut off and the inhabitants of the castle can be deprived of water. At such a time, even a bitter water source inside the castle is better than the sweet water outside. (*Masnawi*, 6: p.134)

The speech of an imitator can be likened to an echo coming from rocks. It is lifeless. Rumi tells us that true knowledge is based in revelation, and it does not die:

"How can a mountain itself produce sound, O naïve one? That sound is the echo of somebody else's voice. Your borrowed words are like an echo coming from the rocks, as are all your attitudes. If your words begin to flow from a source within, only then you will fly with your own wings. Look at an arrow which flies with wings that belong to someone else. Does it have a share of the bird it hunts? A falcon hunts in the mountains, but because it is dependent on others, the king eats both the partridge and the starling it catches. Any words that do not have their source in the Revelation are mere fancy. They are like dust which just disappears in the air. The words of Prophet Muhammad, however, do not disappear, since his words did not stem from personal fancy or wishes. He was a means for the Revelation of God Almighty." (6: p.175)

– What I understand from our talks is that knowledge is not an aim in itself. It serves a much greater purpose. So what is that higher purpose?

– We call it maturing, or "being."

– Then tell me of the steps of "being."

– "Being" means being as God likes us to be. To achieve this, one needs to abandon bad habits and become adorned with good ones instead. Realizing all of these requires strong faith, of course.

V. Your Duty in This City: Being Purified and Becoming a Matured Person

– So let us begin with the importance of abandoning bad habits. But there is one thing I would like to learn first: what is the point of maturing? What does a matured person gain?

– Given that human beings have been sent to this world to behave righteously and become true human beings, they will have fulfilled the paramount duty by achieving this. Through this achievement, they gain, first of all, themselves.

– What does this mean?

– Listen to the *Masnawi* to learn what this means:

You cannot escape yourself

A person who escapes from another stops running when they are safe, far away from the pursuer. However, I am an enemy of my own self, and I hope to break free by running. This is just impossible, as I take myself along wherever I go. Therefore, I need to run without stopping until the Day of Judgment. If a person's enemy is their shadow, they can never be safe anywhere (5:676). O, one of pure breed! Sooner or later, you will lose worldly wealth. But if you become that wealth, the treasure itself, then how will you be able to perish at all? (*Masnawi*, 4:1132)

– Becoming a treasure…So what is the way to be a treasure?

– In order to be a treasure, one firstly needs to see one's own faults and be purified of them. Otherwise, seeing others' faults is of no benefit to us. Actually, the true fault is always to see the fault in everything. Can a person whose soul journeys through the realms beyond see other people's faults? (*Masnawi*, 1:2074)

– So the major fault is seeing faults all the time. That's interesting.

– Right, seeing others' faults can be a serious problem for a person. Rumi explains how ridiculous such behavior is through an example about prayer:

Men at prayer

Four men in India went to a mosque and started their prayer. When the muezzin came in, one of the men forgot he was at a prayer and asked, "Has the call to prayer been made?" The other one elbowed him, "You have spoken aloud and invalidated your prayer!" The third one spoke to the one who warned his friend, "Poor fellow, instead of correcting the other, take care of your own prayer." The last man was glad that he didn't speak to them. But, he couldn't help saying aloud, "Praise be to God that I didn't invalidate my prayer by acting like these fools." Thereby, all of them invalidated their prayers. (*Masnawi*, 2:110)

– I see—but if no one warns another, how can anyone realize their faults and correct them?

– There is a certain way to warn others. The one who warns should be like a mirror or a pair of scales. Scales measure facts; mirrors will reveal what is real. They will tell you, "It is impossible for a mirror and scales to cheat, so then you should abandon your unrighteousness." (*Masnawi*, 1:138) When the mirror and the scales talk like this, what befalls a person with faults is nothing but to listen to the truth. However, it is easier for us to blame the mirror instead of accepting our own faults. This can be compared to the reaction of the ugly man in the following parable:

The ugly man and the mirror

An ugly man who had never seen a mirror in his life came across a mirror shining on the ground in the middle of the dust. He knelt down to take this bright object, wiped it with the hem of his cloak, and held it before his face. However, he didn't like the ugly face he saw in the mirror. For this reason, he threw it away angrily and said, "What a bad mirror you are! If you didn't show faces as being so ugly, no one would have thrown you here!" (2:98)

– So let's assume that I have reached sufficient maturity to see my faults. Then how should I start educating myself?

– Start your self-education by training your soul, your carnal self. Your soul resembles a pool and your behavior resembles a tap that fills it. What is in the pool depends on what flows from the taps; there can be milk or honey, if this is what flows in. Thus, your five senses can be compared to five taps. (*Masnawi*, 1:39) Actually, Sufism is not a matter of images—rather, it is a matter of finding the essence:

> A real Sufi is one who seeks purity,
> Not one who wears a dervish coat and walks solemnly. (Masnawi, 5:364)

Namely, we cannot expect a person to present exemplary behavior without an essential change deep inside. So we need to start by struggling against the carnal self: "The carnal self is the mother of all false-idols. If it is not broken, it will give birth to a new idol everyday. Idols are like sparks, and the carnal self is like iron and flint-stone. The spark will disappear in water. However, iron and stone do not disappear in water, and thus you may be kept safe; the fire is hidden in that stone and iron. As for evil, it is hidden in your carnal self." (*Masnawi*, 1:32)

Our deeds can be compared to the water in a jug, but the carnal self is like a river, for it runs continually:

"The water in a jug or a flagon will run out. But the water from a fountain runs on and on. A pebble will break a hundred jugs, but it can't upset the water from a fountain. Breaking an idol looks easy, but it is pure ignorance to perceive the breaking of the carnal self as an easy task." (*Masnawi*, 1:32)

– Now comes a parable to show how difficult it is to train the carnal self; having confidence in our ability to do this is a deception.

The story of Barsisa

Among the children of Israel, there was a man named Barsisa who was famous as an ascetic. If he blew on water in a glass, the water would heal people. He became so famous that the doctors could find no one to treat. Satan was grinding his teeth in anger, but he could find no way to lead Barsisa astray. He summoned his children and asked, "Is any one of you capable of saving me from this trouble?" One of them said, "I will save you from it." Satan said, "If you can achieve this, then you will be my favorite son, and you will enlighten my blind eye." The young devil racked his brains, but he couldn't find any better way to tempt Barsisa than with beautiful women. He thought that gold or food was only a one-sided desire, for these have no free will that desire in return. But when you love a woman, she may love you, too. It is hard to pierce a wall from one side only, but if two people try from both sides, the hole is made faster. Having made up his mind, he searched throughout the world and, at last, he found a girl who was beautiful and noble enough to serve his purpose. It was the king's daughter. The devil reached into her brain and made her insane. The doctors were helpless. The devil came near them disguised as a dervish and said, "If you wish for her to recover, then take her to Barsisa, and let him blow upon her." They did what he said, and the girl recovered. Thus, the devil passed himself off as a wise adviser. Then the devil seized her brain again, and this time, she was even more ill. He came as the same dervish again and said, "Take the girl to Barsisa again, but this time, she needs to stay near him until she recovers." Prophet Muhammad stated, "If a man and a woman are together privately, Satan is their third." The ascetic man made a great mistake by underestimating his carnal self. He let the girl stay with him, and while she stayed longer, they became intimate. Now the girl was pregnant, and the ascetic was surprised at what was happening, losing himself in deep thought. The devil came near him as a friend and asked what had happened. On hearing the case, he advised the ascetic to kill the girl and bury her, blaming her illness for her death, so Barsisa did as the devil advised. The devil went to the king and told him that his daughter had recovered, while Barsisa was saying that she had died and he had buried her. After this, the devil approached the king in the form of another man and revealed what Barsisa had done. Barsisa denied everything, but the devil showed them the spot where the girl was buried. When they found her body, Barsisa was sentenced to death. While he was being hanged, the devil came near him and said, "All of these things happened to you because of me. Now if you prostrate before me, I can save you." Barsisa asked, "How can I prostrate when there is a rope around my neck!" The devil said, "Even a symbolic movement will do." So Barsisa tried to bow, but the rope hurt him badly. Then the devil said, as stated in the Qur'an, "I cannot respond to your cry for help…" (Ibrahim, 14:22). The company of the carnal self, the devil, and evil friends are only with us up to the gallows—they cannot help us in the grave. (*Majalisi Saba*, 62-71)

– This is a thought-provoking story indeed. Then, if training the carnal self is not easy, it can be seen as the criterion for the quality of a person.

– Correct. Here is a parable that presents us with an alternative perspective on being a king or slave:

Do you consider yourself a king?

The king of a country told a sheikh, "You are poor man. Ask me anything you want, and I will help you." The sheikh reacted: "What an inappropriate suggestion! Although you are a slave of my two slaves, you dare offer to help me! Shame on you!" The king was surprised: "Strange…who are your two slaves who are my masters?" The sheikh replied, "One of them is anger, and the other is carnal desires. They are the only slaves who obey me, but you have become a slave under their command." (*Masnawi*, 2:54)

– So what makes one a true king is freeing the self from the command of desires. Does Sufism require anything else?

– Another important principle in Sufism is being a "child of time," which denotes a high degree of time-consciousness.

> *Take each moment of life as a fortune granted—*
> *Neither worry about the past, nor fear the days ahead.* (82)
> *A Sufi is a child of time—he appreciates it,*
> *Respects it like his father and serves it.* (Masnawi, 3:54)

"Serving time" means completing what needs to be done, without procrastination. Every bad habit resembles a thorn, and one who delays to remove it will be deceived like the man in the following parable:

The thorns

A man planted thorns on a road. As the thorns grew, they began hurting the feet of passersby and ripped their clothes. The governor of the city told him to remove the thorns that were troubling the people. The man, however, kept putting off the task, saying that he would handle it later. Years passed like this. One day, the governor told him, "Day-by-day, the thorns have grown stronger, whereas you are getting weaker. If you cannot extract them now, how will you ever do it in the future?" (*Masnawi*, 2:45)

– This is so meaningful, but why do we fail to see our faults? And even if or when we see them, why can't we remove them immediately?

– If a person keeps committing evil deeds, such deeds become a part of their character, and they don't appear so bad anymore. However, when one with a clear essence commits a sin, they seek immediate forgiveness.

– But if goodness comes first in the essence of human beings, then how can a person's conscience even tolerate evil?

– The conscience is very sensitive when the first evil is committed. Yet if evil thoughts and deeds become recursive, the conscience loses its sensitivity, as happened in the story of Azim.

The story of Azim

A man named Azim from the children of Israel left his home with an evil intention. He came across a man trying to lift a big rock. Azim began watching him curiously. The stone was heavy and it wouldn't move. The man brought another rock and put it on top of the first one. Then the two stones began moving a little. When he brought a third rock, he lifted all of them easily this time and went away. Azim was surprised. How could a man who was unable to lift a single rock carry all three of them? He arrived at a city on the way. He saw an old man at the gate, and he told the old man about the strange case he witnessed. The old man spoke, "Those stones represent sins. A man's first sin is heavy in his view, and he cannot bear it. A second sin makes it lighter. And after the third, they become habitual. (*Majalisi Saba*, 113-115)

– After some time, sins become habitual…and later?

– Be they good or evil, habits become internalized in the long run. That is, the evil becomes not an evil but a need. Such a person will see a thorn as a rose and musk as pitch—just like the leather master who fainted near perfumery shops, as in the following story:

Why did the craftsman faint?

There was a leather master in Konya. He processed leather all day, and it gave off a revolting stench. One day, he happened to pass near the perfumery shops. The poor man was thunderstruck, falling down in the middle of the street. The people around ran to assist him; they unbuttoned his shirt and brought perfume to help him come round. As they redoubled their efforts, the man simply got worse. They didn't know what to do, so they sent someone to inform his relatives. Then the man's brother came running and he immediately understood what was wrong. First, he dispersed the crowd which had gathered. Then he produced a piece of manure, secretly, and let his brother smell it. The unconscious man inhaled deeply, and he got up refreshed. And so it is seen that even dirt can become a vital need.

Likewise, a carcass can be disgusting for people, but it can be delicious for dogs or pigs. The *Masnawi* compares a sin to a stain on
iron. If it is not cleaned immediately, it begins corrupting the iron,
eating it up slowly. Also, lines written on a white sheet are easy to
read. If scribbled over, the obliterated lines will become a meaning-
less ink stain. If this is allowed to go on, the paper will turn coal-
black, like an unbeliever's heart. (*Masnawi*, vol 4, 12)

– But we believe that no one is infallible except for the
Messengers which God sent to people. So we should make a distinction between committing a sin and making sinning a part of
our nature.

– Certainly. We have been given an instrument to wipe away
ours sins, namely repentance. When the Prophet Adam experienced
a "lapse," he was forgiven. Satan, however, insisted on perpetual
rebellion, and so he became accursed. So being a good person does
not mean never committing sins at all; rather, it means turning to
God in repentance right after any occasional mistake one may make
and taking refuge in His infinite mercy. Yet, although repentance is
good, it is not correct to keep committing sins, simply relying on
repentance and, thus, abusing it. Actually, when he saw the sea
closing in on him, the Pharaoh, who was chasing Moses and his
people, fell prostrate, but it was to no avail. One must repent
before it is too late.

– Now, I think I have an overall idea of the way to maturity.
What comes next?

– Before we proceed any further, let's remember what we said
at the beginning. We talked about a servant who was sent into this
world, and the Master Who assigned him to this place. So far, we
have been trying to become acquainted with the servant. Now let
us take a look at the servant's relationship with the Master.

– What is this relationship based on?

– The relationship between God and His servants is based on
two essentials: faith and worship. First of all, one needs to have
faith in God so that one can fulfill His commands. Therefore, in
both the *Masnawi* and in other works by Rumi, we find topics deal-

ing with the existence of God and whether His existence can be recognized though reason—as well as issues related to faith, such as religion, the prophets, divine scriptures, and destiny.

V. Faith and Its Essentials

– My first question is whether God can be known through reason or not.

– Rumi answers a conditional "yes" to this question. Reason needs evidence; however, God doesn't need any evidence. Even though the essence of God cannot be known, the works of God can be appreciated with reason. The following story explains this point.

Where is health?

An atheist philosopher became ill and he went to a believing doctor to be cured. The doctor asked, "What do you want?" The answer was, "health." The doctor advised, "Then tell me what it looks like, so that I can go and get it for you." The philosopher was surprised: "But it cannot be seen, so I cannot describe it like that." The doctor continued, "Then how can you ask for something if you cannot tell what it looks like?" The philosopher responded, "Well, even if I cannot say that, I know that when someone is healthy, he is vigorous and cheerful." The doctor insisted, "But I asked about health itself." And the philosopher concluded, "I cannot tell you, for it is not visible to us."

After this parable, Rumi says, in a similar way God Almighty cannot be described, but His works are apparent. Look at the earth and the sky. How did clouds "learn" to make it rain, and how did the earth "learn" to grow plants? Then know that there is Someone you can't see Who makes what you see happen. Likewise, God Almighty is exempt from needing a voice, but He makes His word heard through every letter, word, and language. This can be compared to the following example: there are fountains near caravanserais. In these fountains you see the figure of a man or a bird. The water seems to emit from the mouth of that man or bird, but everyone knows that it comes from a different source. (Furuzanfar, 57)

Although all these narrations pose a kind of argument, why does Rumi refuse to try to prove the existence of God through reason?

– Knowing God through proof does not maintain lasting faith. A wise person who knows God with their heart is always with Him. Why should someone need to prove the existence of the Being that they are always with? Rumi gives another example: a man knows that the house in which he lives was built by someone. He also knows that it was built by somebody who possessed vision and capability, someone who was alive, and so on. Yet he forgets all these so quickly and thinks only of the house. The wise one however, recognizes the Master who built the house, serves Him, spends his time with Him and therefore needs no evidence, so that master never disappears for him. (Furuzanfar, 67)

On the other hand, reason has a limited comprehension of God; it can bring only you up to a certain point. Rumi explains to what extent reason serves us, and where it becomes helpless: You say that the sea has been contained in your water-skin. This is impossible. Instead, it would be more correct if you were to say, "My water-skin has been lost in the immensity of the sea." Reason takes you up to the threshold of the Absolute Ruler. When you arrive there, however, you should abandon reason, as from here on it will be harmful. There you should just leave yourself to God. For instance, your reason can take you up to the tailor's shop, but once you arrive there, you need to let the tailor work and stop using your reason. Or you can go up to a physician's door, but once you arrive there, you should let the doctor speak. (Furuzanfar, 168)

How can God be comprehended by reason alone? His essence is beyond comprehension, and the manifestations He works appear differently in every instant. For example, despite being a creature of God, you yourself are in a different state, have a different appearance, at every instant. God, too, has a different manifestation at every moment (with all His Attributes and Names as the Divine

Being). For instance, when you feel joy, sorrow, or fear, His manifestations in you are different. (Furuzanfar, 170)

– So this means that reason and faith are not in conflict, but one takes over where the other one ends.

– That is correct. In fact, Rumi objects to the practice of trying to prove God's existence through reason; he takes it as a kind of insolence. Here is the reaction of Shams:

I have proven God's existence

Shams heard someone say that he had proven God's existence with certain evidence. The next day, Shams spoke cynically, "Last night, I heard the angels speak to one another. They were saying, "Thanks to God, this man has proven God's existence and we have not been deprived of Him. All our prayers and glorifications have not been in vain after all." O you man! God does not need to be proven, He is ever existent! It is *you* who needs to prove your position and degree before Him! This is what should happen! (Furuzanfar, 138)

– What an appropriate lesson. And while some people say they believe in God, they have difficulty in accepting God's constant control over the universe. What does Rumi say about this?

– Indeed, just declaring faith in God is not enough. This faith must be prevalent in every aspect of your life. One of the points Rumi insistently emphasizes is that you should not ever associate partners with God. For instance, some take the apparent causes which are the means of our sustenance to be the real provider. So they effectively become a servant for a servant of God. Rumi protests those who exist in almost every era that seek to gain worldly rank or status by servile flattery and the abandonment of human dignity. Rumi explains it thus:

"God Almighty created kings like a small door. Those who attach their hearts to this world do not prostrate before God, but only before the door. Yet only the meanest of people would bow before dogs. And while a cat rules over mice, how can a cowardly mouse be worthy of having the fear of the lion in its heart?"

Believers pray to their "Almighty Lord," but fools take other servants as lords. You boot-licker! If your provider is that lowly man, go ask for his help!" (*Masnawi*, 3:114)

– So those who fail to serve God become a servant for another servant. God's Messenger said, "Sa'd is *ghayyur*,[15] I am more *ghayyur* than Sa'd, and God is more *Ghayyur* than me." God has absolute authority, and sharing His kingdom is absolutely out of the question. Here is a parable to clarify that:

The lion, the wolf, and the fox

A lion, a wolf, and a fox became friends and they went hunting. Actually, the lion didn't need the other two's help at all, but he condescended to this company, for they needed him. The lion hunted a wild ox first, then a goat, and then a rabbit. Then he turned to the wolf: "O wolf, I am so hungry! Come and tell me who deserves what." So the wolf started dividing the prey: "The ox becomes you, for you are our biggest. The goat is of suitable size for me. As for the rabbit, it is more than enough for the fox." The lion flew into a rage and killed the wolf with a single blow. Then he turned to the fox and said, "Let us now see how you would distribute it." The fox immediately fell prostrate and said, "O king, the ox is good for your breakfast. You'd better have the goat for lunch. And the rabbit can be your evening snack. And if you grant me any remnants, I will be grateful." The lion liked this manner of distribution and said, "Well done, O fox! From whom did you learn this beautiful distribution?" The fox pointed at the lifeless body of the wolf, saying, "From that fool lying there." Then the lion said, "Given that you knew your manners, and that you understood that there cannot be two kings who rule, then all three may be yours. I don't need them." (*Masnawi*, 1:119)

– So we are supposed to acknowledge His absolute authority, simply for the sake of His good pleasure with us?

That's right. Here is one more parable:

Thanksgiving to God

Once God Almighty commanded Moses: "Thank Me in a becoming way." Moses asked, "O Lord, how can a servant thank you in a becoming way?" God Almighty declared, "If you consider that whatever comes to you—be it mercy, difficulties, blessings or calamity—comes to you as equal, you will have thanked Me in a becoming way." And, at another time, God told Moses that He loved him. So delighted by this honor, Moses asked, "O Lord, tell me what it is that You like in me, so that I will do it more." God Almighty answered, "When a mother beats her child, he takes refuge in his mother again; he doesn't seek others' compassion. Seek refuge with Me in goodness or evil. This behavior of yours makes Me well-pleased with you." (*Masnawi*, 4, p.112)

– Is there a further step to gain God's good pleasure with us?

– Yes there is. In order to see the ultimate point in this respect, listen to the following parable:

No one is better off

Bahlul Dana once asked a dervish, "How are you? How is it going?" The dervish replied, "Imagine such a man for whom everything in the world happens as he wishes; I am that man. Everyday, the sun rises and sets as I wish; at night the stars twinkle as I wish; rivers flow in the direction I wish—life, death, illness, and health, all of them are as I wish them to be. How could I ever be better off?" Bahlul Dana asked, "But how is it possible for them to happen in compliance with your wishes?" The dervish gave a very meaningful answer: "Given that all of these happen as God wishes them to, and given that I am pleased with whatever God decrees, then I take whatever He wishes as my own wish. In this way, everything is exactly as it should be!" (*Masnawi*, 3, p.72)

– This must be the ultimate level of submission to God. Then I can ask another thing. I understand that faith saves the Afterlife of the believer. But does it serve any good in this world?

– Of course it does—more than you can imagine. Man is weak and he needs a strong shelter, to love, and to be loved. He can find all these only in God Almighty, the True Eternal Companion:

Even if you have everything, without God you have nothing.
While if you have nothing but you are with Him, you have everything.
(Masnawi, 3:1214)

How far can your parents' friendship continue?
Except for God, all friends will leave you. (3:552)

– As the couplets above suggest, relying on the faith of other people is in vain. So, are we supposed to be pessimistic about everybody and everything?

– According to Rumi, no. He found some aspect of beauty in everything. Since, as God Almighty states, there will come such a day when a person will run away from his family (Abasa, 80:34-36), then if a friend turns away from you in this world, do not cry or complain—do not act ignorantly or make a fool of yourself. May be you should give to charity to express your gratitude and say, "Fortunately, what would certainly have happened has not been put off but has happened today. It is so fortunate that I have seen this person's real face before I wasted my entire lifetime in this relationship. I bought some faulty cloth, but thanks to God, it has been noticed quickly. Otherwise, I would have lost my capital and gone bankrupt, and I would have received counterfeit coin in return for my possessions, only to return home happily as a fool. Thanks to God the money has been revealed to be counterfeit before my life was wasted." (*Masnawi*, 5:61)

In conclusion, as far as they are a means to lead you to the Beloved One, all misfortunes are goodness and mercy in reality, because:

If what leads you to the Beloved does not seem pleasant,
Then it must be a blessing in disguise. (Masnawi, 4:80)

– That's a different way of looking at things. Is there a parable about it?

– Of course! And here it is:

The preacher who prayed for bad

There was once a preacher who prayed with gratitude for all sinners, disobedient servants, and bandits. The congregation protested, saying, "What a strange practice; it is not appropriate to pray for those who have gone astray." The preacher replied, "I have benefited greatly from them, and that is why I pray for them. They have been so bad to me that they have taught me how valuable goodness is. They have reminded me about what should I rely on. And when I am tempted by this lowly world, they beat me and curse me and, thereby, they make me turn to the Almighty to seek refuge. So how can I not pray for them?" (*Masnawi*, 4:5)

Every foe is a cure for you, in reality. You run away from each one, and thus seek refuge with God. But your friends, who keep you busy with things other than god, are your actual enemies. Believers are like a badger skin: as it becomes finer when it is conditioned, they become more beautiful as they suffer more. They get more beautiful as they endure more. This is why the Prophets suffered so much. In conclusion, the calamities that come from the Eternal Friend are good for you, even if you don't recognize it. And actually, evil people are beneficial to others, harming only themselves.

– So what is the attitude we need to adopt in the face of troubles as faithful servants?

– The troubles we face in life are mostly what we bring upon ourselves through intention or neglect, but they all are a part of the test we go through as servants. It is important to realize that some seek the help of others in times of trouble. Rumi compares such people to dogs: "Even a dog will not leave the master who feeds it, and he stays loyal to the master. Turning to the doors of others is ingratitude for the blessings granted by God. Even a dog is ashamed of being faithless—so how can you forsake fidelity?" Rumi exemplifies the meaning of a servant's fidelity with a beautiful parable:

Being a servant

A poor, hungry, and half-clad dervish happened to stop in the city of Harat. Roaming through the city, he saw a group of nobles in silk clothes, riding on a special breed of horses. The dervish wondered who those nobles were and asked a passer-by, "What land do these lords rule?" The man replied, "Which lords? What do you mean rule? They are the slaves of the chief treasurer of Harat." So the dervish made a comparison between them and his own miserable condition. Then he looked up to the sky and said, "O Lord, look at Your servant and look at the servants of the treasurer of Harat! See how he provides for his own servants." After a while, someone accused the treasurer of some misdemeanor and the king had him put in prison. He tortured him in order to make him reveal where the treasure was. On seeing that the man wouldn't talk, he then tortured those elegant servants to make them speak. Although their flesh was torn apart with iron vices and their bodies were broken into pieces, none of the servants betrayed their lord. That night, the dervish heard a sound from nowhere, "O wise man! You should learn how to be a servant from those slaves!" (*Masnawi*, 5:128)

– So devotion has a price.

– Yes, but if this price is paid to the One you should pay, then there is no loss at all. Rumi explains to whom people should devote themselves:

"How fortunate is the one who can devote his life and body to the One worthy of it! Everybody is devoted to something, lives for something, and dies for the sake of that thing. A fortunate man devotes himself to such a blessed cause that even his death is a means of life for hundreds of others." (*Masnawi*, 6:3552-54)

– Undoubtedly, an important article of faith is belief in destiny. What is Rumi's understanding of destiny?

– Let me first elaborate on destiny, then talk about Rumi's views. Existence is programmed by its Owner. Not even a leaf will fall outside of God's will. We call what the Divine Will decrees for

His creation as "destiny." However, a superficial eye which fails to see the Divine Will beyond the apparent causes perceives the wind that shakes the leaf as the one who commits the action. Rumi explains this superficial perception with the following example:

The ants

An ant saw a pen moving on the paper, and he started praising the pen. Another ant had keener sight. He told the latter, "Praise the fingers that are holding the pen instead; for I see that the fingers merit the praise." Another ant, which had even keener sight than the first two, said, "I will praise the arms, for fingers are just parts of the arms." And this went on and on...The pen has no power of its own to write on the page. (*Masnawi*, 2:48)

– If whatever happens is the work of a Single Hand, then how can we explain the presence of opposites in the universe? After all, there is good and evil; beautiful and ugly; and so on.

– According to Rumi opposition is only in appearance; for in reality, there is an all-embracing universal order. Every being plays a role in this order. All of us, whether we are aware of it or not, are included in this order. Rumi gives an example of how everyone contributes to the universal order: "A horse keeps treading on an endless belt, but its aim is neither to obtain water nor oil. It only treads out of fear of its master's whip. And an ox gets under the yoke not to do the work but to avoid being beaten. Fear has been given to them by God Almighty so that they will work for His servants. Likewise, the pursuer of every task does not necessarily do it in order to contribute to the world, but rather commits the action for himself; yet in the end, he serves the general order with what he does." (*Masnawi*, 6:83) When a king's tent is to be pitched, some bang the pegs and some tie the ropes. Each one cares about their own particular duty. Yet all of them have the common aim of seeing the king sit in his tent. Thus, God grants a pleasure to every servant in his duty. If all the weavers became viziers, then everybody would remain naked. (Furuzanfar, 140)

Many people, like Zamahshari, wrote volumes of interpretations of the Qur'an, and they produced brilliant sentences. Their aim was to demonstrate their skills, but as a result they served Islam. People aim to satisfy their lust; God, however, aims at the continuation of this world. This way, even if their aim is different, people serve God's purpose, even with their lust, and without knowing it. (Furuzanfar, 156) Similarly, the heat in a Turkish bath is produced in the boiler room. Hay, wood, and manure are the means for producing it. Although they appear to be base or foul, they are actually a blessing for the bath keeper because they constitute the matter that heats the bath and benefits the public. (Furuzanfar, 16)

Rumi applies the same logic to good and evil, and he draws the following conclusion. If an artist draws two different kinds of pictures, some of these being the pictures of beautiful people and others of ugly people, they both display his artistic capacity and neither displays the ugliness of the artist. If the artist were not to draw the ugliness he saw, then the picture would be incomplete. Thus, God creates the deeds of both believers and unbelievers. Therefore, both belief and unbelief point to his Lordship. (*Masnawi*, 2:92) In turn, everything is good with respect to God, although maybe not in our perception. Nevertheless, in the land of a king, there are hangmen, dungeons, executions, and killing along with property and possessions; all are necessary and good. But how can the public consider a robe of honor or execution as being one and the same? (Furuzanfar, 45)

Supplication

O God! A rich man can be very generous. But his generosity can never be comparable to what You give. The rich man donated a hat, but You bestowed an intelligent head. He donated a coat, but You bestowed an entire body. He gave me gold, but You bestowed me hands with which I can count the gold. He gave me a mule, while You bestowed me the intellect to ride on it. He gave me a candle, but You gave me eyesight. That rich man gave me food, but You bestowed me the mouth with which to eat it. He gave me wages, but You bestowed me a life. He gave me a house, while You bestowed the sky and the earth; in Your house, he and several others live and grow fat. What is more, the gold he gave me actually belongs to You, for after all, he did not create it! You are the giver of our bread, and You are the one who gave him bread. You bestowed upon him his generous behavior—it is You made him so generous—and You increased his joy when he acted generously. (*Masnawi*, 6: 117)

– I can understand that hope is necessary in the relation of human beings with their Creator, but why is fear necessary?

– Let me answer this by quoting Rumi: "Someone told me, 'Hope is good, but what is fear for?' I replied, 'Show me hope without any fear, or fear without any hope!'" For instance, you sow wheat. On the one hand, you hope that it will grow; on the other hand, you fear that a disaster will destroy it. Hope is the wing of man— you fly high in accordance with the size of your wing. Why would a patient swallow bitter-tasting medicine if he did not have any hope of recovery? (Furuzanfar, 114) In the following parable, Rumi underlines how hope should overcome fear:

Who is right?

The Prophet Jesus would smile much, but the Prophet John would cry much. One day, the Prophet John asked Jesus, "Are you safe from the wrath of God? Is that why you are smiling like this?" Jesus replied, "Are you crying like this because you cannot put your trust in His mercy?" A saint who witnessed this prayed, "O God, which of these two has a more exalted rank?" And a voice from nowhere replied, "He who hopes for My mercy is superior to he who fears Me." (Furuzanfar, 73)

– One thing that troubles many people's minds about destiny is that God has created everyone with a different potential and a different share. Some see this as a kind of injustice.

– Rumi explains why God gives differently to everybody: "Man can be compared to a tray bearer who presents what God grants. The store is full of products, but there are only a few samples on the tray: a little pepper, a little gum, a little sugar, etc., since the tray cannot hold everything. Likewise, human beings have been given a portion of speech, knowledge, reasoning, generosity, and the like, so that they can trade with them. Yet the treasures of all these merits belong to God, and the people are street vendors, bearing trays filled from God's treasure. Vision or hearing is not limited to our ability; rather this much has been given to us for it is what we can handle. Saying, *Surely we belong to God and surely to Him we are bound to return* (Baqara 2:156) means that we belong to Him as His creatures and servants, as does everything we have; everything comes from Him. He is not visible to us, but His works can be seen on the tray. For example, you cannot see the spring wind, but when it blows, you observe that it is active in all the orchards and fields, and among the flowers... They all come from His heavenly light. (Furuzanfar, 92)

As for other blessings, they are granted to everyone in accordance with their needs. God decrees in a verse that, *There is not a thing but the stores (for its life and sustenance) are with Us, and We do not send it down except in due, determined measure* (Hijr, 15:21). Rain has no end, but it falls every season as it should. Candies are abundant in the shop, but they are given to you in accordance with the money you have. They break off chunks of sugar for you according to how much you can carry. The amount given to one who comes with a bag is not the same as that given to one who comes with camels. Some people are not satisfied with the sea, whereas others are contented with only a few drops. Everything comes to people in accordance to their worth and need. Anything given which is more than one's need or ability is not a blessing. So while love is good, Farhad and Majnun suffered from excessive love, and the Pharaoh went astray because of his abundance of worldly wealth. This is how words are, for they come out to the degree required by the listener. A listener is like flour in the hands of a pastry-master, and words are like water. They add as much water to the paste as the flour needs. (Furuzanfar, 43-46)

– I think the same goes for the readers of Rumi; everyone learns something different from him.

– Right, he explains this as follows: "Our words are like the water controlled by a lock-keeper. If the keeper abandons his post, how will the water know which land to irrigate? Should it flow toward the field of cucumbers, or onions, or cabbages, or to the rose garden? One thing I know is that if abundant water pours from my mouth, then there is a large amount of land to irrigate. If it pours little, then there is only a little piece of land. It is stated in a *Hadith Qudsi*[16] that God grants the power of speech to a preacher in accordance with the need of the listeners. I say that I am a shoemaker, but I cut the leather according to the size of your foot. I have plenty of cloth, but I cut it to fit your body. Take a tiny animal living under the ground with no eyes or ears. Do you think God didn't give it eyes and ears out of stinginess? It just doesn't need them. If something is given to someone without any need, it will be a burden. For example, if you take a carpenter's tools and give them to a tailor, they will only be a burden for him. Like that tiny animal under the ground, some people don't need to the have the eye of foresight or hear the sound of reason, for they do not long for the countenance of God. But these blessings are needed by those who long for the realms beyond. Why should they be given to someone who doesn't wish to have them?" (Furuzanfar, 162)

– When destiny is mentioned, people also remember human free will. Some put the blame on destiny when things go wrong. What does Rumi say about this?

– According to both Rumi and all of the Sunni Muslim scholars, what makes unbelief an offense and what makes worship a merit is man's free will. God does not burden a person with anything they cannot bear, and He holds people responsible only for what they can accomplish. Let's take a look at an example from the *Masnawi* about trying to justify one's offences through fatalism:

– A thief told the guard who caught him, "Whatever I did was decreed by God; I have no fault in it." Then the guard hit him on the back with his stick and said, "Then make sure that whatever I am doing right now is within God's control.!" (*Masnawi*, 5:124)

– So far, we have covered different aspects of faith with reference to the views of Rumi. I have a final question. Nowadays some tend to see Rumi in a super-religious position. Are his ideas compatible with such comments?

– It is as if Rumi foresaw such claims and has already given his answer: "I am a servant of the Qur'an and the dust of the Prophet Muhammad, the chosen one. If I am quoted otherwise, I will plead against those words and those people." All of his works, *Majalisi Saba* in particular, are full of *naat*s—poems expressing his love for the Prophet. Further, Rumi expounds in detail on the *hadith* which states the importance of following the Sunna of the Prophet: "At a time when the Muslim community breaks with Islam and consequently disintegrates, the one who holds firm to the Sunna gains the reward of a hundred martyrs." (Furuzanfar, 12)

Also, according to Rumi, who refers to the *Hadith Qudsi* which states that God created the universe for the sake of the Prophet, all of the prophets and saints are like a part of the Prophet's shadow. Even if a shadow enters a house before its owner does, the one who enters is still the owner of the shadow. Therefore, even if the previous prophets came earlier, this is only a relative priority. No matter what one's organs do—hands, feet, or others—any merit goes to the intellect. Likewise, Rumi explains that all the rest of the prophets' merits actually belong to the Prophet Muhammad, for whose sake the universe has been created. (Furuzanfar, 158)

– So how does he view other religions?

– Islam stipulates the acceptance of all other prophets along with Prophet Muhammad. In terms of being the final divine religion, Islam perfects all other religions. The quotations below summarize Rumi's thoughts on this issue:

This is what we learned from our fathers

"Christians say that they follow what they learned from their fathers and refuse to accept Islam. So tell me, if you inherit a counterfeit banknote or fake gold from your father, wouldn't you readily exchange it for pure gold? Or do you consider it superior, for it has sentimental value? Likewise, if you inherit from your father a crippled arm, would you refuse a doctor's help as this is something you inherited from your father? Or, if they offered to transfer you from the diseased wasteland where your father lived and died to another land with fresh air and water, would you still stick with the old one? God has granted you a different brain, different eyes, and a different ability to distinguish between right and wrong. Don't follow your father's mind, which leads you to nothingness, but follow the mind which leads you to true existence."

Yorash

The father of Yorash was a ragman. When he was taken to the royal court, the king taught him good manners and a special technique for fighting. Yorash didn't say, "I came to this world as the son of a ragman. I don't ask for anything else; open up a junk-shop for me instead." Even a dog abandons hanging around garbage when it becomes the pet of the king. It pursues the new favors it is blessed with. A falcon is that the same. Even an animal will abandon its parents when it finds somebody to take better care of it. It is a great misfortune for people to fall behind animals in this respect.

It would be correct if you say, "Whoever serves Jesus, he will have served God." But if God has sent a Messenger with priority over Jesus, it means that God has revealed much more through him than through Jesus. (Kabakli, 336-39)

Although Rumi invited people to Islam, he was broad-minded and respectful toward other religions, since he was aware that followers of all religions sought righteousness in their own way. From time to time the Greeks of Konya also joined the circle to listen to his

talks, and they benefited from that fountain of wisdom. Even though
they didn't understand Turkish, they felt sadness and joy, and they
even cried—presenting other emotions as well, as they listened. One
man said in contempt, "Even the Muslims here don't understand
these words properly; the crying of the Greeks cannot mean much!"
Rumi replied, "They don't have to understand the literal words.
They understand the essence of my words. They know that the subject is God, His provisions for His servants, His forgiveness, and His
punishment. In these words, they feel the scent of their Beloved One
and feel moved. All people love God and supplicate to Him sincere-
ly. However, the faith within has no name. When faith flows into
molds of words, it solidifies, gains a shape and is named; it becomes
belief and unbelief." (Furuzanfar, 145)

If ten people own a garden or shop, they will be united in their
speech, worries, and trade, for they have the same aim. And on the
Day of Judgment, all people will be occupied with God; they will
all unite with Him. (Furuzanfar, 41)

– After having discussed faith, let us now consider worship,
the natural requirement of faith.

VI. Worship

– There are certain forms of worship in every religion. Why does
God require us to worship Him?

– It is true that God requires us to worship Him. Worship
means a consciousness of one's servanthood. Human beings, who
were given their share from the divine breath, always carry the
potential to claim divinity. In fact, sometimes they forget the real
source of their power and inflate their ego, becoming a Pharaoh.
So worship is both a means of closeness to God and a reminder so
that humans will not try to claim divinity. On the other hand, "A
person's wish for prayer and his fasting all stem from God's attract-
ing His servants toward Himself" (*Divani Kabir*, I:375).
Struggling against the carnal self and fasting are difficult, though.
But difficulty is better than God's rendering a servant distant to

himself. (*Divani Kabir*, VI:1769) Some forms of worship are directly related to social life. Furthermore, worship can be sincere or hypocritical. Rumi comments on the true meaning of worship and what should it contribute to the worshipper:

"The prayer, fasting, Hajj, and struggling in the way of God all bear witness to one's belief. Fasting says 'This one refrained from even the lawful, so he will no way commit the forbidden.' *Zakat*—the prescribed alms—says that 'He even sacrifices from his property, so how can he steal from his fellow believers, his fellow companions?'" (Divani Kabir, V:183, 199) But if they are false witnesses, their testimony will not be accepted at the Divine Court. Hypocritical worship is like the seeds a hunter spreads—nothing but a trap. A cat seems to be fasting but, in fact, it watches for careless prey. To sum up, your worship seems to bear witness to your belief, but the witnesses must first prove reliable. A person who worships otherwise is like her who destroys her yarn that she herself made strong.[17] (*Masnawi*, 5:9)

– So in what way should we worship, if it is to be accepted by God?

– Rumi compares worshipping to planting a seed or a sapling. You plant a sapling for the sake of eating the fruit, and you sow seeds for the sake of obtaining those crops. But does every seed germinate, or each sapling yield fruit? Of course not. There must be essence in the seed so that it can germinate, and the sapling must be that of a fruit tree so that it can yield fruit. One who plants a fruitless kind of sapling, or sows a seed without essence, will waste his own efforts. According to Rumi, the indication of sincerity at worship is the spiritual pleasure you feel; its salt and pepper is yearning and love. Otherwise? Otherwise, our condition will be like that of a treadmill which turns without knowing what it does. In terms of rotation, a treadmill and a pilgrim turning around the Ka'ba are alike; but one of them is engaged in an unconscious act, whereas the latter is participating willfully, with a clear aim. Just as these two are not the same thing, so the two kinds of worship we have mentioned seem alike but cannot be equal with respect to their natures. So, too, real worship is being oblivious of everything before God. Rumi gives another example of this. One day a king told a virtuous dervish, "When you are honored with a manifestation of God, remember me, also." The latter said: "At those moments, I cannot remember my own self, let alone you" (Furuzanfar, 20). This kind of worship is welcome in God's view. If God chooses a person and melts that person's ego into His own being, He fulfils the wishes of those who follow that individual, as well, along with the person's. This can be exemplified as follows: A king had a special slave. Before he was admitted to the presence of the king, petitioners would write down their wishes and hand them to the slave so that he would present them to the king. But the slave would become unaware of everything but the king when appearing before him. So when the king wondered what the slave wanted, he would search his pockets. Then he would find the petitions and write his orders so that their needs would be fulfilled. (Furuzanfar, 20) So, what is meant by worship is loving God and fully submitting to Him, though the outer form of worship may change in different religions.

– How does it change?

– Before the Prophet Muhammad, prayer and fasting did not have the same form, but the previous religions did have some forms of prayer and fasting. There was the essence of the Qur'an at the time of Moses and Jesus, but it wasn't in Arabic. So the meaning is what is maintained. For instance, when you say that medicine has an effect, you describe recovery but not the form of medicine. (Furuzanfar, 113)

"Worship and remembrance of God are fans that revive the fire of faith in one's heart. But if there is no such fire, worship and remembrance are like blowing upon ashes (*Majalisi Saba*, 74). The same is true for reading the Qur'an. A *hafiz*—one who has memorized all of the Qur'an—who doesn't understand what he recites is like a child playing with a walnut. What makes the walnut valuable is the nut and the oil it contains. But if you break the walnut to give to a child who is playing with the walnut, he will reject these; a whole walnut as a whole makes a noise, but the nut and oil don't.

The Companions of the Prophet virtually "ate" the Qur'an. It is difficult to eat even a large body of bread, but if you just chew the bread and spit it out, then you can eat the bread carried by hundreds of thousands of donkeys. This is the case with a person who recites the Qur'an but doesn't understand or abide by it. These are the people who are addressed in the *hadith*, "There are such people who recite the Qur'an that the Qur'an curses them." (Furuzanfar, 122)

– Some say that the love of God in one's heart is sufficient and that they do not have to worship further. Is worship through mere love, without any words or a certain order or form, valid?

– According to Rumi definitely not. "All meanings appear in a certain form. Faith is in the heart, but if you don't affirm it with your words, you won't be considered to have faith. Prayer is an action, but it won't be valid without reciting verses from the Qur'an. So it is mistaken to say that words and form don't have value." (Furuzanfar, 113). In the following couplets, Rumi describes worship as a witness of love and as a gift from one friend to another:

> *If love (and worship) were only thought and idea,*
> *Then fasting and prayers wouldn't be incumbent upon us.*
> *Friends present gifts to one another as a sign of attachment and love—*
> *Those presents are witnesses of love and attachment.*
> *There's sincerity and togetherness hidden in them—*
> *Such offerings are the concrete witnesses of the love formed in the heart.*
> (I:2725-28)

– So which kinds of worship does Rumi emphasize most?

– He emphasizes two types of worship in particular: prayer, the way to human ascension, and fasting, which is another divine blessing. According to Rumi, there are two types of prayer: the first type is the five daily prayers, and the other is the prayer that covers 24 hours. The first belongs to an ordinary believer, while the latter belongs to the lovers of God.

– Then what did the Prophet mean when he said, "Two units of prayer is better than the world and what is in the world"?

– Rumi explains it as follows: "The hadith points to those who lay so much importance on prayer that two units of prayer is more important for them than losing the world and everything in it." (Furuzanfar, 28)

– Is there anything more valuable in the world than prayer?

– When someone in his circle asked the same question, Rumi answered thus:

"Faith is more important than prayer because prayer is prescribed five times a day, whereas faith is required all the time. There may be certain excuses for lapses in the former, whereas there is no excuse for lapses in the latter. Prayer without faith doesn't help, but faith without prayer will help. Also, prayer can be different in every religion, but faith doesn't change in any." (Furuzanfar, 46)

– You mentioned the "prayer of lovers." What do you mean by that?

– In the couplet below, he describes what he means:

> If you can see through the eyes of wisdom,
> Both worlds manifest the divine kingdom. (Masnawi, 6:3261)

– Then it means that no matter what we love, we actually love God. Have I understand it correctly? My second question is why does God show His manifestations behind veils?

– These are two important questions. Let us listen to the answer from Rumi:

"A person's love, directed to a thousand things, like his parents, spouse, friends, properties, etc., are all a veil. After leaving this world and seeing the Ultimate King, without any veils, everybody understands that all their wishes were just a blind—and, in reality, it is only God they long for. So why does the King manifest Himself behind such veils? The answer is as follows. We see, walk around, and get warm thanks to the sun. The sun makes fruit sweet and it makes crops grow. But if the sun were to get a bit closer, then it would burn and incinerate us. When God Almighty manifests Himself through veils, mountains are adorned with hyacinths and tulips; but if He manifests Himself without any veils, even mountains like Mount Sinai could not bear it." (Furuzanfar, 50) And even if God is beyond these veils, being constantly in prayer results in seeing God everywhere. According to Rumi, then, manifestation is to a real lover what water is to a fish: "Though the daily prayers are only five, true lovers are in constant prayer. For the intoxication in their head will not be satisfied by hundreds of thousands of prayers, let alone the five daily prayers. A moment of separation is like year to the lover; and a year of togetherness is like a dream! Love is also thirsty; thus, it seeks the one thirsty for it. And so it is that love and the lover follow one another, like night and day. Love is within the lover himself. Nobody can tell his own self, "Visit me a little." Likewise, nobody can befriend himself in turns." (*Masnawi,* 6:2684)

– This sounds like bringing Paradise to earth.

– That is how it is. Nevertheless, as Rumi says:

"If you are a lover, listen to my words! Being high or low is with respect to the lover. You can even be in a pit, but if you are close to Him, you will know that you are on a heavenly throne. Without Him, even if you are in the heavens, you will be at the lowest level; for love is Paradise, and Paradise is where the lover is. Paradise without the lover is Hell. One who owns it lacks for nothing. As for those without Him, their existence is like a mirage. Then don't care about rank or status—care only about being near the beloved." (*Masnawi,* 3:4555)

– Now I have an idea about prayer. So what does Rumi think about fasting?

– Rumi, who ate little all through his life, and who sometimes ate as little as once in three days, gives special importance to fasting. He describes it as a divine blessing, the vividness of one's breath for the spirit. The following lines from his poems are particularly noteworthy for the different perspectives in which fasting is examined. They enthusiastically voice a love of fasting:

"Ramadan has come—the flag of the King of love and faith has arrived! Now keep away from material foods. Spiritual sustenance has come from the heavens, and a feast for souls has been laid. The soul has been freed from the load of the body, and the demands of our nature have been blocked. The army of love and faith has come, and it has devastated the army of deviation and unbelief! In this way, fasting is a sacrifice for our salvation; thus, our soul attains a greater life through it. Our carnal self, which commands us to commit evil deeds and to commit sins, desperately needs to be purified. When Ramadan comes, the door of the prison of sins is broken; the soul is freed from captivity of the body; thus, it ascends to the heavens and reaches the Beloved!

In the days of Ramadan, hang onto the rope of mercy which has descended, and save yourself from the imprisonment in the well called "the body." Prophet Joseph is near that well, calling you, so be quick and lose no time! When Jesus saved himself from his bodily desires, the wishes of that donkey called the physical body, his prayers were accepted. So you, too, will be purified from your bodily desires. Wash your hands! For a heavenly table full of spiritual food has descended!" (*Divani Kabir*, I, 459)

"Consider fasting as something that holds a surprising potential! Fasting gives you life, and it grants you a heart. If you want to see something surprising, then be surprised about fasting!

– If you wish to ascend to the heavens, know that fasting is an Arabian horse brought before you.

– Fasting blinds bodies so that the eye of the soul is opened. The eye of your heart is blind; therefore, your prayers and your worship do not bring you the light they should—they do not show you the truth.

– Fasting takes away the animal side of the animal in a human shape. This is why fasting is necessary for the maturing of the human side of a person.

– The life of lovers has been darkened because of the kitchen called the "body." And fasting has come to light up those kitchens.

– Is there anything else in the world which resembles a dagger ripping open the devil's stomach—anything which is more of a devil-slayer, better to shed the blood of the carnal self?

– What is there, at the door of the King of kings, with a secret and special duty, and which yields benefits so quickly? What do you think? Fasting, of course!

– Fasting refreshes longing hearts so much that even water is not as refreshing to a poor fish!

– When an initiate starts struggling with the carnal self, fasting contributes more than hundreds of thousands of helpers in the path of reaching the destination of the heart.

– The structure of Islam is based on five pillars: the declaration of faith, the prescribed purifying alms, pilgrimage, fasting, and prayers. I swear by God that the strongest, and the greatest of them is fasting![18] In each of these five, God Almighty has hidden the meaning of fasting. The value of fasting is hidden in the same way that the night of Qadr is hidden.[19]

– Fasting is like a ring or a crown through which God grants His loyal servants the kingdom of Prophet Solomon. He lets his most special servants wear it.

– The laughing of a faster is better than the state of a non-fasting person in prostration, since fasting will allow him sit at the table of the All-Merciful.

– Although you do not realize it, when you eat food, your insides are filled with filth. Fasting is like a bath. It purifies you from material-spiritual filth and all evils.

– Have you ever seen a beast honored with the light of knowledge? The body is still that of a beast. Do not follow the beast by abandoning fasting!

– You are like a drop separated from the sea of God's unity. How will you return to your origins? There you are—fasting takes you to the sea like a flood, like the rain.

– When you start fighting with your carnal self, say, "I won't easily abandon fasting!" Then throw yourself on the ground, clap your hands, stamp your feet, and resist!

– Your carnal self is like an invincible warrior threatening the heart, but fasting makes it shake like a rose petal.

– They talk about a darkness which holds the water of life. For thinking minds, that darkness is fasting. If you wish for the light of the Qur'an to be in your soul, know that fasting is the secret of the pure light of the entire Qur'an.

– Pure people sit at heavenly tables, the tables which appeal to the soul. Here is fasting—it lets you eat from the same bowl with them.

– Fasting makes you one whose heart is bright as the day, whose soul is as pure. Then it sacrifices your being on the day of reunion with the King; it saves you from existence and ego.

– When you have reached the month of fasting, welcome it in a cheerful mood, thanking God for having reached that blessed month! Since fasting is bad for those who are sorry for the coming of Ramadan, who are grieved by it, they are not worthy of fasting. (*Divani Kabir*, II, 803)

"O heart! You are a guest of God when you fast; heavenly tables become you! You have closed the gate of Hell in this blessed month. Therefore, you open thousands of doors leading into Paradise!" (*Divani Kabir*, III, 1326)

– Truly, these examples are an expression of such a deep love of fasting that it is unequalled in all of Islamic literature. But now, I have a question about worship. I have often noticed that some people think the following: "Given that I fulfill all the requirements of worship, then I will surely be saved in both worlds!" Is this really so? Is the worship we do an exchange for the blessings we enjoy in both this world and the Paradise?

– Goodness, no! How could such a thing be possible? Worship can never be an exchange for blessings; it can only perhaps be a means for them to be granted to us. The following parable is a beautiful example for this point:

The return of worship and a jug of water

There once was a Bedouin family living in the desert. One night, the Bedouin's wife whined, "O my husband, what will become of us? How much longer are we going to suffer poverty? I have heard that there is a just and generous Caliph in Baghdad, and the city is like springtime thanks to his generosity. They say that he never turns anyone down. Why don't you go there and present our condition. I hope that you will not return empty-handed." The man replied, "Alright dear, but I cannot go there without a present! In order to ask for something, you are supposed to take something there. Yet we don't have anything becoming that palace!" The woman thought for a while and she found something: "We have the rainwater in our jug! How can they find such pure water in the city? It will make a good present. Now let me clean and seal the top of the jug, and then you set off on the road for Baghdad." Before narrating the story further, I would like to note that the jug denotes the body, and the water denotes worship, servanthood, and knowledge of God. And the king? Undoubtedly, that is the owner of the realm of existence. Then what is the Bedouin doing? Whose water will he be presenting? Whose possession will he be offering? In short, he wasn't very convinced by the idea, but there seemed no other way to satisfy his wife, so he set forth. He passed the desert with great effort, and he made his way to the palace. When he was admitted into the royal presence, he was treated kindly by the king, who accepted his gift and ordered his men: "This water is so valuable; each drop of it is worth a gold coin. Empty the jug right now and fill it with gold. Then take our guest back to his home through the river!" The poor Bedouin took it literally and he said to himself, "So my wife was right! The water I brought is such a welcome present!" But when the servants took him to the boat near the immense Tigris River, he was fascinated by the depth and clarity of the river. Then he bent toward the water and took a handful to his mouth; it was more delicious than sherbet! So he felt ashamed by what he had previously thought. "Poor me! Woe to my poor understanding! Here is a great and sweet body of water running near his palace. Is such a king in need of the bitter and muddy water in my jug? I take it that his acceptance of my present was to honor me and to bestow gifts upon me without disgracing me! So he made his blessings look like a return for what I had brought (*Masnawi,* 1:91)

All of these bring us to the following conclusion. Our worship and prayers cannot be a price to be paid for admittance to Paradise and the Countenance of God. The Owner of this universe does not need what we offer Him. He accepts our worship as a pretext for granting us Paradise, that is all. A truly wise person is one who knows this. Therefore, it was said:

> *The ascetic trusts his deeds and confidently sleeps,*
> *But the eyes of the wise ignore all his deeds.* (Majalisi Saba, 124)

– Supplication to God is also a form of worship, is it not?

– Of course it is. We can even say that it is the essence of worship. But the most excellent supplication to God is the one made for another person. The way to attain it depends on making others pray for you by the favors you do. The following parable exemplifies just that:

The mouth which never committed a sin

Can a person pray through another person's mouth? It does not seem possible. Once, in order to show Moses how this could be, God Almighty commanded him to supplicate to Him with a sinless mouth. When Moses said, "I do not have such a mouth," God commanded, "Then you supplicate to me with another person's mouth. You cannot have sinned by another person's mouth." Moses said, "O Lord, how can I supplicate to you with another person's mouth?" God answered, "Make effort to do goodness to people and gain their prayers for you, so that several mouths will pray for you night and day." (*Masnawi*, 3:8)

What a beautiful prayer!

VII. Return to the Friend

Now let us remember the servant we mentioned at the beginning. He was sent by the king to this world with a special assignment. At last, the time is due for him to return. Here, we are about to conclude our questions and answers. So, how was the servant to return so that he would be welcome?

Rumi states that humanity was the reason why the universe was created. Just as the purpose of planting a tree is to have fruit, so too, the raison d'être of the tree of creation is its best fruit: the mature human. Although the roots, branches, and the leaves of the tree all emerge before the fruit, the fruit is still more valuable than the rest. This is the case with humans with respect to the other creatures and their coming into existence. (*Masnawi*, 2:36-37)

If man matures and turns into a servant who is becoming to his Lord, then he will realize his purpose in creation. But success or failure is evaluated by an examination. A farmer's success is judged at the time of harvest, and that of man is judged at the moment of death, the time of harvest for him. Thus, this is how Rumi explains the wisdom behind death:

Why are people allowed to die?

One day, Moses dared to ask God, "O Lord, You have created so many beings so beautifully, and then they just perish by the Angel of Death's scythe. What is the wisdom behind that?" God Almighty replied: "Do you want to know the reason? Then go and plant seeds in your field. You will have the answer at the time of harvest." When the time came, Moses started cutting the crops with a sickle and grinding them into flour. Then he heard a voice from nowhere: "O Moses, why are you cutting and destroying the crops you grew?" Moses said: "I cut them so that the grains are separated from hay; so that the wheat will go the granary, and the hay will go to the haystack. I did it to make a distinction." God Almighty said: "And I have created death and the Judgment Day, the harvest time for souls, so that the mature and the raw will be separated, that the good will be distinguished from the evil." (*Masnawi*, 4:115)

– At harvest time, wheat is favored so much, whereas hay is stamped underfoot. Then death must not be so difficult for those whose soul is like wheat to be offered to the Friend.

– Naturally. What is horrible is not death but our real face surfacing upon the mirror of death—for death has no color of its own. It shows the beautiful as beautiful, and the ugly as ugly. The beautiful wait for the time of death eagerly. In their eye, death is their reunion with the Beloved, for when what you will get in return is something far more valuable than your life, death becomes a profitable trade. Rumi explains it thus: "Life is dear only when there is nothing dearer. When there is something dearer, then life loses its value; it becomes secondary." So one does not hesitate to exchange one's life for something worthier. Rumi narrates the following event about the Prophet Muhammad's uncle, Hamza:

Death as Hamza views it

In old age, Hamza began to join battles without wearing armor. Onlookers remarked, "Even in your younger and stronger days, you were always cautious, and you wouldn't fight without armor. Now, despite the fact that you are older, you are so careless. Why don't you follow the command, 'Do not get yourselves into danger with your own hands'?" Hamza replied, "In those days, leaving this world seemed to me like annihilation, like being thrown into a dragon's mouth. Nobody wants to throw himself into a dragon's mouth. But now, I seek death as seeking a beloved one. Death is not such a danger for me and I do not want to run away from it. To whomever death is a danger, let him run away from it and follow the command 'Do not get yourselves into danger with your own hands.'" (*Masnawi*, 3, p.131)

Thus, when the ugly face of death changes, the state is no longer death. Even if it appears to be death, it is actually a reunion. (*Masnawi*, 3, p. 177) If you put a caged bird in a garden, the poor bird wishes to join the other birds outside. It yearns to be let out to the garden. Even if it cannot achieve that, it sticks its head or its foot out of the cage with the desire to be free. But if there is a cat waiting in ambush just beside the cage, then afraid of losing its dear life, it wishes there were a hundred more cages upon its cage.

So those who fear death actually fear what follows death. (*Masnawi*, 3, 151)

The behavior of Hamza helps us understand why Rumi referred to death as "the night of reunion." But what exactly will God require when we go into His presence?

He asks for nothing but our own selves. We have previously mentioned the difference between being something and having something. God Almighty, the True Owner of everything, will look at what we are, not at what we have, and then judge accordingly. We will take there nothing but our own selves, our own heart, and our own soul. In order to explain how nothing else counts at that door, Rumi narrates the event between Prophet Solomon and the Queen of Sheba.

Bring me yourself

When the Queen of Sheba received the Prophet Solomon's letter inviting her to submit to God, she understood that it came from someone important. Instead of accepting the invitation, she wanted to please him with gifts, so she sent forty camel-loads of gold. However, when the envoys taking the gifts arrived in Prophet Solomon's country, they were surprised to see that even the roads were paved with gold. They considered turning back since they felt ashamed, but they carried on to fulfill their duty. Prophet Solomon spoke to the envoys, who were brought into his presence: "These things you have brought are only good for ornamenting the necks of our mules. What I care about is not the gifts but yourselves. Anyway, you do not actually own these goods, but they are only in your temporary possession. These things cannot be truly owned by any of us—they just keep circulating. In addition, I do not expect any wages in return. My reward will be with God. So bring yourselves as presents. Remove the worship of heavenly bodies from your hearts, and have faith in God." (*Masnawi*, 4:25)

Likewise, God Almighty demands of us that we submit ourselves, devoting all our heart to Him. According to Rumi, God

Almighty will ask us on the Day of Judgment whether we have anything to offer Him, or whether we came as we were created, without bringing anything to offer. Then He will reveal that what He cares about is not good speech, nice clothes, or the properties we own. He cares only about the beauty and purity of our hearts—whether we are spiritually beautiful or not. (*Masnawi*, 2:1776) With these words, Rumi relates the following verse:

> The Day when neither wealth will be of any use, nor offspring,
> But only he (will prosper) who comes before God
> With a sound heart. (Shu'ara 26, 88-89)

God only expects us to come before Him with a sound heart which is free of all kinds of unbelief, hypocrisy, and the association of partners with Him.

– And a "sound heart" is like a pure and bright mirror?

– That's right; a purified heart is like a bright mirror. It is the best present, as neither the earth nor the heavens can contain God Almighty—but He tells us that He can be contained by His servant's heart. Thus, there is nothing better than a beautiful heart which becomes a mirror for divine beauty. In this regard, Rumi provides the following parable:

I have brought a mirror to you

A friend of the Prophet Joseph[20] came to visit him. Joseph asked him, "O dear friend, what is the present you have brought me?" His friend felt ashamed. He began crying and said, "You have abundant wealth, and peerless beauty! I thought for so long, but I couldn't find a suitable gift for you. Whatever I were to bring, it would be like presenting a particle to a mine, or a drop to a sea. If I have a seed in my hand, your stores are overflowing with them. Your beauty is unsurpassed in this world. Therefore, I have brought a clear mirror to offer you. O you, who makes the sun in the sky envious! What can be more beautiful for you than watching your own beauty?" (*Masnawi*, 1:126)

How glad are those who can take such a mirror to their Lord!

Finally, in the Words of Rumi

WE HAVE COME

We have come—
With words yet untold,
And with faces full of mercy for people.
We have sensed the yearning of hearts,
And we have come with tongues that transcend any tongue.
We have come,
Taking the sky above us as our home,
And all people as our family,
And we have adopted colorlessness as our color.
We have taken the seventy two nations as our siblings.
We have come.
Others came and left—
They lived, died, and disappeared.
We have been born, never to die,
And we have come, never to leave.
We have come,
In order to pour everywhere like the rain,
To enter every house like the sun,
And to touch our face to people, like the earth.
In short, to love and be loved,
We have come.

NOTES

1   Khidr was a blessed person whose parable is narrated in the Qur'an (Kahf 18:60-82).

2   The word *sama,* which literally means "hearing," is a Sufi form of prayer by whirling. Rumi would feel enraptured with divine love; he would begin to whirl in submission to the Creator and in harmony with creation.

3   In Sufi literature, the symbolic character Majnun stands for an initiate. He falls in desperate love with Layla.

In the long run, the initiate's transitive love turns into divine love. Thus, love of Layla is a metaphor for love of God.

4   The initial chapter of the Qur'an.

5   A saying of the Prophet Muhammad.

6   The term *shabi arus* literally means the "wedding night." Rumi used this metaphor to imply that dying means returning to God; therefore, for a believer it is a happy occasion to be celebrated.

7   In Sufi terminology, *chila* denotes a period of suffering when an initiate spends at least forty days in strict austerity and self-discipline in the name of spiritual training.

8   In the parable, four men who speak different languages—a Turk, an Arab, a Persian, and a Greek—disagree on what to buy. In fact, they all wish to buy grapes but they just don't understand each other. (Ed.)

9   Say: "He, God, the Unique One of Absolute Unity. God, the Eternally-Besought-of-All (Himself in no need of anything). He begets not, nor is He begotten. And comparable to Him there is none." (Ikhlas 112:1-4)

10   A form of poetry in Eastern Literature.

11   The Archangel Gabriel

12   This word which means "cut off" refers to the Qur'anic verse: *...it is the one who offends you who is cut off* (from unceasing good, including posterity). (Kawthar 108:3)

13   Abu Jahl was the head of the Meccan idolaters and the archenemy of the Prophet. (Tr.)

14   Wine is a well-known Sufi metaphor for "divine love." It is sometimes taken literally and misunderstood in the West.

15   (Muslim, *Lian*, 17) When used for people, the word *ghayyur* (jealous) defines a man who is very sensitive about the chastity of his beloved wife. When used for God Almighty, it states that God Almighty never shares His Kingdom with anyone.

16   This is a specific category of sayings from the Prophet. The wording is the Prophet's, but the meaning belongs to God. (Tr.)

17   *see* Qur'an (Nahl 16:92)

18   Fasting is considered superior to other types of worship in terms of acknowledging our weakness, poverty, and impotence before God Almighty and understanding our position as His servants.

      The night of Qadr occurs in the third part of the holy month of Ramadan. Spending that night in devotions is of great worth.

19   The Prophet Joseph was the most beautiful human being ever created in terms of physical appearance.

BIBLIOGRAPHY

Abdulhakim, Halife. *İslam Düşüncesi Tarihi* (The History of Islamic thought), trans. Yusuf Z. Cömert, ed. M. M. Şerif, Istanbul. İnsan, 1991.

Aflaki, Ahmet. *Ariflerin Menkıbeleri* (Parables of the Sages), trans. Tahsin Yazıcı. Hürriyet, 1973.

Arpaguş, Safi. "Mevlana Celaleddin Rumi'nin Eserleri Üzerine Yapılan İngilizce Çalışmalar" (Studies in English on Rumi's Works), *Tasavvuf Dergisi*— Mevlana Özel Sayısı (The Magazine of Sufism—Rumi Special Issue), 2005.

Can, Şefik. 1995. *Mevlânâ: Hayatı Şahsiyeti Fikirleri* (Rumi: His Life, Personality, and Thoughts). Istanbul, 1995.

———*Divan-ı Kebir - Seçmeler* (Selections from Divan-i Kabir). Istanbul, 2000.

———*Mevlana, Rubailer* (Rumi, quatrains), The city of Konya Ministry of Culture, 2006.

Ceyhan, Semih. "Mesnevi," *TDV İslam Ansiklopedisi* (TDV Encyclopedia of Islam), vol. 29. Ankara, 2004.

Chittick, William. "Rumi ve Mevlevilik," (Rumi and the Mevlevi Order), trans. Safi Arpaguş, *Tasavvuf Dergisi* (The Magazine of Sufism), Rumi Special Issue, 2005.

Cumbur, Müjgan. "Mevlana'nın Eserlerinde Türk Boyları ve Türk kelimesinin değerlendirilmesi" (An Evaluation of the Referals to Turkish Peoples and the Use of the Word "Turk" in Rumi's Works). Paper in *Bildiriler – Uluslararası Mevlana Semineri* (Proceedings of the International Rumi Seminary) Edited by Mehmet Önder. Ankara. Türkiye İş Bankası. 1974.

Çelebioğlu, Amil. *Mesnevi-i Şerif, Aslı ve Sadeleştirilmesiyle Manzum Nahifi Tercümesi* (The Original Text of Nahifi's Translation of the Masnawi and its Simplified Form). Istanbul. Sönmez Neşriyat, 1967.

Demirci, Mehmet. *Fihi Mafih*, 13:58-59. DVIA.

Demirel, Şener. *Dinle Neyden* (Listen to the Ney). Ankara. Araştırma Yayınları, 2005.

Furuzanfar, Bediüzzaman, *Mevlana Celaleddin,* trans. Feridun Nafiz Uzluk. Istanbul, 1986.

Göktaş, Vahit. "Mevlana-Şems Münasebetinde İnsan-ı Maşuk Felsefesi" (An Understanding of "The Beloved Person" in the Rumi-Shams Relationship), *Tasavvuf Dergisi*—Mevlana Özel Sayısı (The Magazine of Sufism—Rumi Special Issue) 2005.

Gölpınarlı, Abdulbaki. *Mevlevi Adap ve Erkanı* (Mevlevi Ethics and Manners). Istanbul. İnkılap ve Aka, 1963.

———1959a. *Mevlana Celaleddin,* Istanbul.

———1959b. , "Mevlana Şems-i Tebrizi ile Altmış İki Yaşında Buluştu" (Rumi Met Shamsi Tabrizi at 62), *Şarkiyat Mecmuası,* 1959.

———*Mevlanadan Sonra Mevlevilik* (The Mevlevi Order After Rumi). Istanbul.

Güleç, İsmail. *Türk Edebiyatında Mesnevi Tercüme ve Şerhleri* (The Masnawi's Translations and Explanatory Works in Turkish Literature). TUBA: 2003.

Hasan, Seriful. "Mevlana ve İkbal" (Rumi and Iqbal). Paper in *Bildiriler – Uluslararası Mevlana Semineri* (Proceedings of the International Rumi Seminary), Edited by Mehmet Önder. Ankara, Türkiye İş Bankası, 1974.

Kabaklı, Ahmet. *Mevlana.* Toker, 1973.

Kadir, A. *Bugünün Diliyle Mevlana* (Rumi in Contemporary Language), Gözlem, 1980.

Kafalı, Mustafa. *Cengiz Han,* DVIA. 1993.

Karaismailoğlu, Adnan. *Mevlana Kongrelerine Sunulmuş Tebliğler Bibliyografyası* (A Bibliography of the Proceedings of the Rumi Symposiums). Konya: 1996.

Koner, M. Muhlis. *Mesnevi'nin Özü* (The Essence of the Masnawi). Konya. 1961.

Köprülü, Fuad. *İlk Mutasavvıflar* (First Sufis). Ankara. (1919), 1966.

Mazioğlu, Hasibe, "Mesnevinin Türkçe Manzum Tercüme ve Şerhleri" (The Masnawi's Turkish Translations in Verse With Annotations). Paper in *Bildiriler – Uluslararası Mevlana Semineri* (Proceedings of the International Rumi Seminary), Edited by Mehmet Önder, 275-297. Ankara, Türkiye İş Bankası, 1974.

Melikoff, Irene. "Batı Hümanizmasının Karşısında Mevlana'nın Hümanizması" (The Humanism of Rumi Versus Western Humanism), *Mevlana: Yirmi Altı Bilim Adamının Mevlana Üzerine Araştırmaları* (26 Researchers on Rumi), (ed. Feyzi Halıcı), Konya, 1983.

Rumi, Mevlana Celaleddin. *Mecalis-i Seba* (Majalisi Saba—The Seven Pieces of Advice), trans M. Hulusi. ed. M. Doğan Bayın. Istanbul. Kırkanbar, 2001.

———*Mecalis-i Seba, Mektubat*—Seçmeler, (Selections from Majalisi Saba and Rumi's Letters). ed. Abdulbaki Gölpınarlı, The City of Konya Ministry of Culture, 2006.

———*Mesnevi* (Masnawi). trans. Veled İzbudak. Istanbul, 1988.

————*Divan-i Kebir* (Divani Kabir—The Great Divan). ed. Abdulbaki Gölpınarlı, Kültür Bakanlığı, 1992.

————*Fihi Mafih*, trans. Meliha Ülker Tarıkahya, Maarif Basımevi, 1954.

————*Mesnevi ve Şerhi* (The Masnawi and Its Explanation). Ankara. Turkish Ministry of Culture, 1989.

Nicholson, R. A., *Mevlana Celaleddin Rumi*, trans. Ayten Lermioğlu. Istanbul. Tercüman Gazetesi.

Okuyucu, Cihan. *İçimizdeki Mevlana* (The Rumi Within Us). Istanbul. Bilge, 2002.

————2006. *Mevlana Konuşuyor* (Rumi Talks). Istanbul. Bilge.

Önder, Mehmet. *Mevlana Celaleddin-i Rumi*. Ankara, 1986

Önder, Mehmet, İsmet Binark, and Nejat Sefercioğlu. Eds, *Mevlana Bibliyografyası*. Ankara. Türkiye İş Bankası, 1974.

Öngören, Reşat. *Mevlana*. DVIA, 2004.

Ritter, Helmut. *Celaleddin Rumi*. vol. III. IA, 1993.

Sahih Ahmed Dede, *Mevlevilerin Tarihi* (The History of the Mevlevis), ed. Cem Zorlu, Istanbul, 2003.

Schimmel, Annemarie. 1992. *I am Wind You are Fire: The Life and Work of Rumi*, Boston.

————2002. *Aşk, Mevlana ve Mistisizm* (Love, Rumi, and Mysticism), ed. Senail Özkan. Kırkambar.

————1993. "Mevlana Celaleddin Rumi'nin Şarkta ve Garbta Tesirleri" (The Influence of Rumi in the East and the West). Paper at the Sixth National Rumi Conference, Konya.

————1978. *Mevlana ve Yaşama Sevinci* (Rumi and the Joy of Living), ed. Feyzi Halıcı. Konya. Konya Turizm Derneği.

Sipahsalar, Faridun. *Mevlana ve Etrafındakiler* (The Risala of Sipahsalar), trans. Tahsin Yazıcı, Istanbul. Tercüman, 1976.

Sultan Walad, *Ibtidaname*, trans. Abdulbaki Gölpınarlı. Ankara, 1976.

Şems-i Tebrizi (Shams of Tabriz). *Konuşmalar: Makalat*, trans. M. Nuri Gencosman. Istanbul, 1974.

Yaylalı, Kamil. *Mevlanada İnanç Sistemi* (The Belief System of Rumi), Konya.

Yakıt, İsmail, "Mevlana'ya Göre Hayatın Evrimi" (The Stages of Life According to Rumi), Paper at the Second National Rumi Conference, Konya, 1987.

————1993. *Batı Düşüncesi ve Mevlana* (Western Thought and Rumi). Istanbul. Ötüken.

Yazıcı, Tahsin. *Divan-i Kebir*, 9:432-433. DVIA, 1994.

Yeniterzi, Emine. *Mevlana Celaleddin Rumi*. Ankara. TDV: 1995.

INDEX